# R E M E M B R A N C E

## A . K E R E S C H

FOR Z, S and J, who opened the door.

# REMEMBRANCE
A. KERESCH

Copyright © 2016

Publisher: GMB Press

Layout by bayugraphic (*bayugraphic@yahoo.com*)
Cover Design: *Flight From Babylon* by Sacha Stone

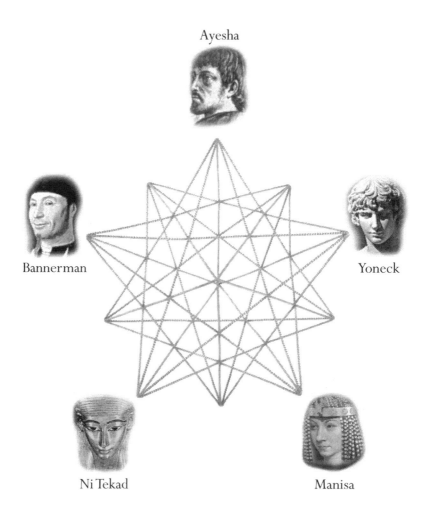

Ayesha

Bannerman

Yoneck

Ni Tekad

Manisa

The author writes in the framework of myth, history, imagination, remembrance, and personal experience over a long lifetime of living between the seen and unseen, illuminated with guidance from extraordinary people. This book is not channelled.

# CONTENTS

*The Alien*

*A tall Karesch once,*
*perhaps an Uzbek,*
*I called fate through the stones,*
*and told men what they know*
*but chose to forget.*

*When tired of reading thrown stones,*
*I walked by waters dark green*
*where cries of wild geese*
*tore tears from my throat,*
*and I rose to the skies*
*behind the pale moon*
*beyond the star lines*
*to far crystal climes*
*of sun-splintered light.*
*No shadows, no time.*

# Foreword

Come with me through the mirror into another world. Sit with me by star fire where tales of wonder will take you deep into your heart, give your mind wings, and awaken vistas in your intuitive imagination. I tell of times past, passing, and to come, for we, the Keresch, have been involved in your evolution over eons, with our presence helping to guide and guard you as inconspicuously as possible. We are all woven into the cloth of gold that is Life throughout the Multiverse. We too have made mistakes. We too search for truth in your world and ours. As if holding a candle we know there are no definitive outlines, only approximations floating like shimmering shapes in the space observed.

In her era, the wise Edwardian writer, Dame Ivy Compton-Burnett, once remarked:

*"You can't teach anyone anything that they don't know already."*

But one can remind people of what they have forgotten, and what lies sleeping, dreaming like the princess immured behind castle walls in the fairy tale. So permit me to speak in myth and metaphor, to give meaning, but not always explanation. You may ask if this story is true.

Should it be so 'on your terms' in order for it to be of value to you? Do the Keresch really exist?…Yes. Can you prove it?…No.

Why is the story being presented? To remind those who can be reminded of what they have forgotten. If it is not always understandable, then feel it, don't just think it.

Weave your own reality from symbols, ideas, and feelings beyond the words that you read. Weave them up, over, under, and along the warp and woof of your inner life to create your own garment of glory.

Travel well with curiosity. Remember, you will arrive safely.

# Introduction

The narrative is confined to the memories of an intergalactic, inter-dimensional Keresch warrior who has chosen over the eons to incarnate or manifest in this world as the means of teaching Earthlings to recall their spiritual heritage and understand the structure of their psyche. In a framework for reiterating much ancient knowledge and putting it in the perspective of our present modes of scientific thought with its remarkable progress in delving into matter and materialism, we nonetheless experience an increasing void when it comes to acknowledging or understanding spirit. Even more unfortunate are the present efforts to turn *Homo sapiens* back into being a slave race so many of them once were, and about which the teller of tales explains. Men could, and can be, gods or demons.

How can mankind go forward if they do not know what is behind them? *Remembrance* covers a vast inner and outer landscape linked by the thrust of transformation that occurs through understanding. Tales are told in the form of the personal experience of this cosmic traveller, whether here or in outer space on the home planet of the Keresch once menaced by dark forces.

The confrontation of polarity is a basic theme throughout the narrative with suggestions for resolution. This is a time *of* change and *for* change due to a unique convergence of the cycles of time and this planet's position in the spiral of our rotating galaxy. Our vibrational field is accelerating as never before.

## THE TREE OF LIFE

The Tree of Life is a universal symbol always exquisitely represented in the art of your cultures. Everywhere this primordial, sentient, changing, living, developing tree, resplendent in many dimensions, is rooted in the heart of earth to grow upwards into heaven. Imagine the roots protecting a great stone. It is a singing stone holding the beating heart of your planet known as Gaia, the universal goddess who nourishes you. Think of the stone as a protective pericardium to Gaia's heart, and similar to a skin it will reflect every external trauma you have inflicted on her together with its internal effects. The resonance between the outer shield of the pericardium and the inner functioning of the heart should be one of harmony. In the case of your planet it is not. Her heart is damaged by your lack of consciousness in the assault on her protective outer covering. Imagine the symbolic figure of Atlas, surely the figure of galactic, cosmic man in his creative functions, holding on his shoulders your world in which he has so long been involved. Suddenly he finds the strain of supporting a sick, stinking globe, too much.

He shrugs, Gaia falls, and…

How many of you understand this situation, either in symbol or fact?

*Homo sapiens* you call yourselves! Man who knows. Man who knows that he knows. Knows what? Is conscious of what? Man should have wisdom because he can reason and has a metaphysical constitution for emotion combined with the magic of intuition, linking animal instinct to the higher human capacity for inspiration. When consciousness is blunted, the ability to experience the higher ranges of vision and thought, love and joy remain beyond reach, and you will be beset by negative entities. They will devour your soul and prevent you from protecting the singing stone holding the heart of Gaia
beneath the Tree of Life.

*Thou shalt find to the left of the house of Hades a wellspring.*
*And by the side thereof standing a white cypress.*
*Do not approach the wellspring.*
*Thou shalt find another by the Lake of Memory cold water flowing*
*forth, and there is a guardian before it.*
*Say, "I am a child of the Earth and starry Heaven,*
*but my race is of Heaven alone.*
*This ye know yourselves.*
*And lo I am parched with thirst and I perish.*
*Give me quickly the cold water flowing forth from the Lake of*
*Memory."*

*Gold tablet of Petelia* 4th century BC

*We ask as Fools who know not our Spirit*

*Where are the hidden traces left by the Gods?*

Rig Veda. Book 1. Stanzaa 164

*The Dream*
*(extract)*

*He held his dialogues; and they did teach*
*To him the magic of their mysteries;*
*To him the book of Night was open'd wide,*
*And voices from the deep abyss reveal'd A*
*marvel and a secret-Be it so.*

*Lord Byron (1788-1824)*

## CHAPTER 1. ORIGINS

I stem from a race as old as time, the oldest warriors of the galaxy. We were seeded from the mind-born Sons of the Fire Mists when the universe was ready for our embodied presence. Our immortal flame, emanating from the central invisible sun of our system, took form by choice in a vibratory frequency that is invisible to you.

Even though through the mirrors of time our bodies became denser, you would still not see us unless gifted with a different sight. I write in myth and fable to give meaning and invoke imagination without always giving comfort in explanation.
As for Time? Let it remain a mysterious ambiguity: does it flow fleet between our dreams, or, unknowingly, do we rush through the stillness of Time?

Behind everything rests an unknown, unknowable mystery of the inconceivably great, invisible, blazing power beyond creation. It was the mystery god of your ancients. From this mystery came Origin that reflected itself throughout the universe, and dreamt the Dreamers who dreamt you and me.

Before the beginning there was a pregnant emptiness, like a vacuum, the zero point dense with potential (not a nothingness since no thing can come from nothing). Therein slept potential, waiting to be awoken by Mind. Co-existing with the active Mind was Sound in Light, the vibration that turned primal passive substance into matter in motion, ready to receive the imprint of dreams from the Dreamers. The Dreamers, a collective consciousness both Dream and Dreamer, projected on the virgin fabric of space the splendours of all realms. Light was their messenger. Homogeneous Light, carrying the information for all modalities of existence, was fractured in its passage through the seven great frequencies descending to your physical universe.

In the 17th century, the blind English poet, John Milton (1608-1674), an initiate, saw with an inner sight the pattern of creation. He transcribed his visions into poetry of ageless significance.

## LIGHT

*Hail, holy light, offspring of Heav'n first born,*
*Or of th'Eternal Coeternal beam*
*May I express thee unblam'd? since God is light,*
*And never in but unapproached light*
*Dwelt from Eternity, dwelt then in thee,*
*Bright effluence of bright essence increate.*

The higher frequencies of the unseen always direct and control the worlds of greater density in a perpetual progress of expansion and contraction, given image in a myth, reputedly passed down orally for over 10,000 years. It tells of the never- ending beat of Shiva's ever-dancing feet. Imagine his hair as the loom, the warp and woof, each holding the pattern in an ikat weave (indicative of the interweaving of electromagnetic waves), defining the birth and death of whirling galaxies as they arise in mists of space, traversed by hissing dragon-serpents undulating in their paths of electromagnetic power.  Shiva the transformer, entwined with snakes, dances in  all the worlds while his brother (some say his son), Vishnu the preserver, stands watching, one eye open in judgment, the other closed in the compassion of the Avatar.

In the texts of your ancient philosophers, the incorporeal Dreamers known as the Logos, working through portals of power, relayed their Light into the universe. The Greeks thought of the Logos as being the seat of the firstborn of gods. These cosmic intelligences, directing the anima mundi of all orbs, from suns and planets to atoms, were the source of a perfect idea that descended into the  distortions of increasingly dense matter. From the first Logos of the Universe, came a hierarchy of Logs directing the processes of manifestation on any level.

Earth's reality is but a fractal of a hyper-dimensional hologram. It is told in the story of Plato's cave where man, restricted to an underworld, only sees things from theoutside cast as shadows on the walls confining his abode. Amidst the glories of sound and light, the Dreamers dreamt Adam Kadmon, the archetype for Galactic Man. In your sacred scripts it is written:

> *The spirit of the eternal shot out from him in blinding sheets of light*
> *and his blueprint was impressed on all the oceans of space.*

You could ask: is this divine archetype immutable, and is it the impetus behind evolutionary change and progression?

Humans, living in the low, slow vibrations on Earth, feel alienated from *Origin*, forgetting that they hold within themselves a portion of the Divine, reflected in the indestructible spiritual principle that can be reached by opening and working through the heart chakra. The heart has the highest electrical charge of any organ in the body. The heart chakra is the seat of your spirit, your *Immortal Flame*. There are other human-like creations in the cosmos that do not have this eternal principle. But this is another story within my myth. So our spirit, the *Immortal Flame*, together with its lower expression, the *Spark of Life*, is common to the Family of Man and your form is embodied in sheaths of different densities all related in circuitry of biochemical electromagnetic paths in a subtle network that has been modified at best and at worst disconnected.

The origins of humans on Earth come from many places over eons of time. Humans have been savaged, fractured and damaged in genetic experiments by intruders from beyond your solar system who have been coming here for many millions of years. My people were some of those, who, although also working in genetics to improve Earthlings, objected to inappropriate, nefarious experiments. We fought on Earth as well as in other dimensions. We sometimes appeared here for a limited time, or incarnated in a body of your human kind to ameliorate what was happening. But having taken part in experiments, for better or worse, it landed a certain responsibility on our shoulders.

Your unconventional researchers claim that around 1,300,000 years ago the

Anunnaki, composed of different types and factions, in manipulating the genes of an early human species you think extinct, produced Heidelberg Man, your ancestor in common who already had a fairly developed mind. Come 350,000 years ago a great leap forward presented the Neanderthal. Their brain, larger than yours today, held deep memory and perceptions that crossed frequencies into dreamtime and communion with Nature that was embodied in a different consciousness forgotten and little understood in your present world.

Then the Anunnaki, around 285,000 years ago, perfected cloning a human slave race to mine gold in Southern Africa. Further change appeared in the next leap ahead, circa 150,000 years back, when genetics corroborate that the Anunnaki, together with other extraerrestrial involvement, altered your species and produced the more self-conscious Cro-Magnon Man. He evolved, rebelled, and ate of the tree of knowledge. For a period the two species co-existed before the newcomer predominated. You could call the Cro-Magnon your "modern man", with facial and bodily proportions conforming to the Fibonacci sequence that did not grace his less elegant but in many ways more gentle and spiritual predecessor.

In covert fashion, the game of genetic alteration continues today with the same opposition once recorded in your myths of the War in Heaven. It tells of certain so- named "angels" who refused to join the experiment when the gods lusted after the daughters of Earth and in intermarriage produced giants, referred to in your scriptures as the Nephilim. Some say they were monstrous, devoid of reason, and had to be destroyed by one of the many floods. Others claim amongst them were heroes, demigods, whose exploits were recorded in the personae of Theseus, Heracles, Jason, and others in Greek mythology, as well as exotic tales from so many of your other early cultures. It was a time when gods, demons, and men intertwined in a ferocious fandango of adventures portraying the human qualities of Earthlings of mixed heritage: you, Homo sapiens. Your will and strength were tested against the arrogance and superior powers of beings with whom you shared a seasoning of their genetic stamp and the same basic elements of matter found in the stars and your toenails.

Your pineal and pituitary glands are virtually atrophied. Your sixth sense lies undeveloped. You will see through a glass darkly until healed by reconnecting the subtle circuits of energy that run through the invisible meridians in the flesh. They link body, emotions, and mind to the full richness of your environment, as well as harmonising your higher faculties to receive the upper range of information transmitted in light. You are aware of only a minute part, less than 1%, of the electromagnetic spectrum in which you live. All the more reason why you should live by your established five senses to the best of your ability. Your outer and inner life depends on them for every sensory perception and their assessment. Remain aware when you touch, smell, see, hear, and taste because they help open you to the sixth sense. They are the gateways to perception. They are the gateways to awareness and although your senses can be fooled, deception is diminished if the information is discerned through the intuition of the heart-brain, the door to higher perception, your link to Source and the first organ to form in the foetus that is acknowledged by your medics to have brain cells within it structure.

We, the Keresch, are far from perfect, albeit an evolved race. An ethereal Fire largely influences the characteristics of our nature. The other great Mystic Elements of Earth, Air, Water and Ether are also within us. They are intelligent energies whose qualities, perceived on your planet like pale shadows of their higher forms, give substance to the fabric of manifestation. Warriors we are, with food unknown to your world. We can, if necessary, replenish ourselves on Light alone, and when we feel our strength failing there are the white caves, vast caverns on our planet with crystals thick as towering trees growing from dark mineral floors, that, during contemplation, absorb destructive influences of a mind out of harmony.

As warriors, the quality of our core is a white Fire relayed from the creative centre of our Galaxy and assimilated through the eye of the sun, a lens for cosmic forces in all solar systems. Born with little fear, it was both our strength and weakness. We resembled tempered steel and had to be near broken before we could transmute our weakness into strength. Our weakness was hubris in thinking we were beyond domination, and obstinacy in refusing to change methods of confrontation when fighting any malicious attack on the Laws of Light. We had, over time, become imbalanced and too polarized.

My tribe, like every Keresch warrior, took a sword, short or long, with a flame-shaped blade as our emblem. When we joined together with others of our race     we were called the Host of Flame, a descriptive name tinged with a pinch of salty fear. Such was our reputation for success in war that it went to our heads, and at one time we suffered because of our ruthlessness. We understood only too well your Jesuits adhering to their choice of the end justifying the means.

"Barbaric mercenaries!" muttered the Galactic Council when our presence was sought by some beleaguered members under threat from the darker realms of activity.

"Should the Council really send in that Flaming Host?" queried the  Head, always given the honorary title of The Crown in a consortium where all were equal, or as you would well comment, some were more equal than others. In addressing the assembly he continued: "These warriors don't mind losing their bodies, but are getting, I think, unnecessarily brutal with the adversaries. They give them no quarter when perhaps a trade in prisoners and our diplomacy might bring more lasting results. After all there are means of persuasion other than attacking the body. We do have our knowledge of the mind, not forgetting, of course, the value of exchange   in what we have perfected, namely, the transmuted metals."

Significantly, this was alluding to  gold  used  amongst  other  things  as  a psychic booster to invoke an inflated perception of the universe. We called this "the expensive explosion for inadequate junkies". Our lack of reverence for many things did not always endear us to mainstream Galactic. They are inclined to take  themselves a little too seriously. A sense of gentle amusement they have; a sense of  the raucously ridiculous they lack. We also firmly believed that this booster, however convenient, did not in the final count develop the inner and higher aspects in man, be he human, extraterrestrial, interdimensional or humanoid, the latter being an unfortunate creature with high intelligence but constituted without the Bridge. Transmuted gold, nonetheless, opened heightened perception and emotional excitement without forging the individual's own psychic muscles to repeat the experience without the gold powder.

"But," continued an aged member of the Council "we are not always successful in enlightening those beings with a psychic constitution lacking the Bridge."

She was referring to our dreadful enemy, our polar opposite, the Cysts, those great reptilian beings, travesties of humanoid form, who waged war of bestial ferocity in that long gone age, still recalled in myths of many nations. I will return to the reference of the Bridge later.

Unluckily for them, the Cysts on numerous occasions had betrayed us. Their cunning was infamous, and their contempt for justice or honour nonexistent. They would agree to a treaty then break it as soon as it was to their convenience. Finally, when requested to fight them we insisted on having it entirely our way. The enemy was to be obliterated. No quarter given. But, in fact, obliteration was impossible. Like the Hydra's head, the Cysts would always reappear, although perhaps in the stream of time they could transform themselves into more awakened creatures. In the meantime, the majority of the Council agreed to let us be autonomous. The aggressive enemy had to be kept at bay and we were the best to achieve the desired result. We also laughed amongst ourselves. The Council had no qualms about getting us to do their dirty work.

In accepting to fight for the Council's federation as much as for our own safety, we asked for no pay or trade with our renowned Black Fire Crystals unique to our planet. We do not employ money as you do. Anything we need we take pleasure in making or we manifest it. We often barter between ourselves, and don't think we don't bargain. We enjoy doing it in a game played with much mirth. On the other hand, information, services, or ideas are not for sale, whereas our metals and crystals are used for commerce with other Galactics who pay in gold. With the Council we only asked for an exchange of information connected with healing. The Crown readily agreed. The first draft of the treaty was signed. The details for the exchange, we were told, would be completed after the battle.

How well I can still bring on to the orb of memory the figure of my Commander. He stood up over seven foot tall, and with customary protocol lowered his head for three seconds before The Crown. The seated assembly of hundreds, each cloaked in purple, slowly raised their right hand in acknowledgment. The high hall, spanned by arched ribs of green stone similar to translucent malachite, suddenly became illuminated signifying the end of the meeting, closed with the Galactic Chant in a long, penetrating harmonic of AUM.

They sent us in with my tribe in the lead. It was my first battle. I was young. This was in the Age of Heroes, so long ago, when your world was in a different frequency, less solid than it is today. The creatures there, together with early types of your humans, were like shades moving on the watery land of Lemuria. You might think of it as being an ancient dreamland into which we could come with ease, as the shells between the different states of vibration were less rigid than in your present time. Earth had not yet solidified into its present form. It lay, a sentient being, protected and nourished by a grid, a web of energies arising from its own consciousness, and nourished by the greater consciousness of the cosmos itself. We agreed to fight the Cysts for our mutual benefit. For this war of vengeance, we perfected lethal weapons with which we gained victory, but it caused us to lose face with the Galactic community. This bitter victory, my first battle, changed our attitude, and led us into degenerate self absorption.

Our pride at that time, although not in fact our downfall, was superseded by an arrogance that overrode all reverence for Cosmic Law. We felt we had the right, as a last resort, to beat the devil at his own game. We decided to use a combination of forces beyond just an emanation to kill bodies. Our weapon could destroy both the physical and astral form of the Cysts, obliterating them into states of darkness for eons until their soul- seeds would be recreated in Darkness from their own font of life. Unlike Man, they never had an eternal flame. The Cysts, and others similar to them in our Galaxy of many entities, knew well how to enslave souls.

Although they could also fry the inspirational and creative superior mind of Man, disconnecting him for a time from his Eternal Being, they could never create this principle aligned to indestructible Spirit. In time, we were to learn the possibility of redemption for their kind. However, we were in that epoch, willing and able to wage war on the lowest of principles in the name of the highest ideals. No wonder the Galactic Council permitted us to do their dirty work! And in this respect, deriding them, we raised our swords to our own glory. Our Keresch legions came chanting, unfurling our tall banners of red purple, and gold. "Beware you Cysts!" we bellowed. "We come with vengeance to annihilate you!"

In times of confrontation we are apt to be theatrical, exhibiting our exuberance for our pleasure and not necessarily to impress our foe. Eight hundred thousand of us readied for war. We went into their dimension and invaded their main planet, arriving by stealth in our long ships only visible after landing. Never to be underestimated, the Cysts were unexpectedly fast in their defence. They struck with the speed of snakes. They used paralysing rays to stop us. We battled with our protective shields, our electromagnetic weapons, and our small, round, airborn globes that released our specialty of total disintegration.

All this took place in a different time, a different reality than that of your present Earth. Where we fought the sky was dark, the overhanging orb, a ball of livid fire, and the earth thick with mud and blood. Smoke from the high pyres swirled upwards in the flames from cremating our dead.

Our warriors, men and women, brought the slain bodies laid on long wagons to be burnt with songs of sadness and praise piercing the roar of fire that bellowed like oxen in the aftermath of battle. The reptilian humanoids, known to draw back under pressure and abandon their own when a fight was going badly for them, were cowards in contrast to our legions. We stood by each other and our commanders to the very end, no matter how bitter it might be. For us life and death were two sides to the same coin washed by time.

How easy it is for me to recall my Commander, also my sworn partner, lover, protector, and teacher. And there I was, so young, at my first battle in the most violent of scenarios. The merciless opponents were coming from all directions while I stood my ground alongside him, the leader of our clan and people, and a man held in awe on our planet. I was relieved to find beside him other warriors of his similar strength and calibre to guard his back and even keep an eye on me, not always sure which of my weapons to use in attack or defence. The initial atavism of my race helped me. I even had moments of pleasure and excitement expanding into exhilaration when repelling those slithering, hissing, screeching humanoids. Other moments near broke my heart on watching playmates and friends die together, never letting out a sound as they fell under the onslaught of the crafty enemy, that if time permitted would tear a Keresch apart for instant food. They towered over us, dribbling yellow slime from their jagged mouths opened over bared teeth.

Outnumbered after three sleepless days, we drew the Cysts into an ambush planned by my Commander. A few hundred of us stood in a circle, shouting to provoke an attack. The rest of our legions lay low in a far wider circle, as if dead, hiding the aura of their life force and the deathly globes under their shields. Once the Cysts responded to our taunts, we bombarded them with our fatal weapon, followed by wielding every possible arm known to combat in those times.

There is great beauty in the martial arts of my race whirling as an avalanche of superhuman strength toward an adversary. The mayhem of slaughter in your wars is so primitive. I suppose you Earthlings will say we excused horror not by what was done, but because of the elegant way in which it was achieved.

Cysts who avoided the globes were hunted down, slain in cold blood, and disintegrated. No hostages. No quarter given. The few that remained, mounted on metal robots, retreated to their underground cities.

We decided not to attack with our diminished forces. Instead we laid waste to the land, and before flying away poisoned the air in their terms for several generations to come. We knew they would breed again. How many and in what time span we could not say having obliterated hordes of an existence in any dimension. We knew we had possibly overstepped the boundaries of war according to the enlightenment of Galactic Man with his indestructible identity of an Eternal Flame not bequeathed to the Cysts from their own genesis. We had hit below the belt at a sentient but deprived species.

Triumphant and exhausted, when my Commander presented himself and our five elders at the Council, I was astonished at our cool reception, even more so when The Crown hesitated in his reply to our request for an exchange in information on healing.

"It was agreed," announced my Commander, "that you would send us your high priests to converse with ours in recognition of the successful outcome of war with the Cysts."

"Certainly!" replied The Crown after a short silence, "Although this may be difficult. Which high priests do you want, Commander Ayesha? For we are all high priests here, are we not?"

At this point our small delegation decided to unilaterally withdraw from the assembly for an unspecified length of time that had an effect on our race for longer than anticipated.

Commander Ayesha stepped back on one foot and made a sweeping, courtly bow, waving his right arm to the floor in a long out of fashion, graceful gesture. With raised eyes he said clearly, "The Crown, I am assured, will understand that we, the Keresch, are unworthy of such prolific praise. Permit me to decline and withdraw in peace." He turned, and, followed by his entourage and me, left the high hall of green radiance in silence before the Council chanted AUM.

In speaking of battle that involves consciousness before and after death, it brings me to the subject of birth, the body, and the Bridge, previously mentioned in our meeting with the Galactic Council for war against the Cysts. So let me return to my family and siblings. I always think of them with satisfaction. We live together by choice in a group, each child, other than the first, having witnessed the return of an ancestor. Were we born? Did we grow old and eventually die? Yes. But not in the way you might think.

---

*Before continuing with this story of Origins, Cosmic Perspectives, Timelines, the Cysts and a Bitter Victory, close the book and retire to think about all the information. It will take a while to digest. Ponder; contemplate the questions that arise in your mind.*

*The phoenix hatched an egg of flame,*
*The egg of eggs from which we came.*

*Keresch children's rhyme.*

## CHAPTER 2.  BIRTH ON OUR HOME PLANET

On our small planet each tribe has its priests, attending to our twelve- metre high birth chambers carved into the Crystal Mountains. The knowledge of these men and women, transmitted in a bloodline, assures a genetic pattern that renews their ancestral abilities. Light arises from a self-induced unseen source. Perfumes fill the air, as the sense of smell adds to the power of sound coming from crystal bowls, gongs, and tubes. Do not think this is old-fashioned. These procedures, once known in your world, heighten the senses in an atmosphere conducive to communicating with other realms. Sound can heal, destroy, or help the process. Mantra, a science nearly lost on Earth, is one of our essential rituals in the Birth Chambers. We have reached the level where, with advice from our priests, we decide which ancestor to contact for reincarnation.

The couple and the ancestor are in  phase with each other on  every level. The polarity of male to female is not disruptive if the two are in harmony. Their love for each other  and  the  incoming reincarnation, their  combined  intention and attention all create a compatible interaction, a harmonic field of mental and emotional energy for communication between two different  states  of  existence. The composition of one dimension must have its reflection,  its  fractal  pattern  acting like a shared memory transmitted through a joint field of awareness that influences future development. You call it a morphic  resonance.

At death the ancestors withdraw to another state with levels harmonically related to our planet, and to which they are most attuned. They remain there until, called by our power of mind and songs of remembrance, they are drawn back by resonance to materialize again in the egg. They come forth as a new reincarnation ready to live with the mutually- chosen family. In the Birth Chamber any power of mind, if orphaned from feeling, if not combined with love, is never successful. Love, like a magnet, attracts the ancestor in another density where he or she has resided between incarnations. In principle, barriers between differing fields of vibration protect us from being attacked by forces greater than our capacity to reject, or from a higher frequency so intense in light that it would shatter us. In your world the protection has become a barrier to diminish your perceptions, and bind you to the stream of time.

You cannot pass 10,000 volts through a structure built to take 100 until it has in some way been transformed, or the incoming voltage lowered. Your brain, for example, acts as a transformer that receives information from a different vibratory dimension accessed when your mind functions in the frequency of theta and lower alpha waves.

Our transformation of energy in the Birth Chambers eases the entry of the incoming incarnation. First appearing as a beautiful sphere of radiating blue light with a small brilliant white aura, the orb remains in the air, waiting for its own impulse to merge into the opaque ectoplasmic egg we have created. The orb enters the egg to develop into its human form warmed with the first principle, the Spark of Life, and ordered by the second principle, the material Lower Mind, with its cellular intelligence announced in the first movement of the foetus. We nourish the body of the returning ancestor passing from another density into our physicality with plasma responsive to embryonic growth. With you Earthlings it takes 49 days for the first sign of the pineal gland, your gateway into psychic viewing, to contain DMT (dimethyltryptamine), a secretion associated in your understanding with hallucinations. Its appearance in the foetus corresponds to the same number of days the Buddhists assign to the errant soul before it enters a new body for reincarnation.

With us, the pituitary, pineal, and hypothalamus glands as well as the heart, are coordinated to beat in tune with the pulse of our planet. Many are the times during embryonic development I have stood with family members and our priests watching and waiting for the moment the body receives the principle of its material Lower Mind with its cellular intelligence and cleverness transmitting biological information faster than light. We sit quietly by the egg, sending our thoughts and love augmented from crystal energy directed towards the evolving body in its preparation to house the identity of the incoming ancestor.

Love is a song or, as some say, it is a state of being rather than a passing emotion. Love is a vibration. It builds bridges between frequencies. Its pitch, beyond your ears, resonates in harmonic waves, coagulating shimmering, invisible, geometric shapes that contain energy for the infrastructure of manifestation. In your world, pass an electric current through a plate with metal filings and watch them assemble themselves into spontaneous patterns. Sound achieves the same result. It can organise or shatter matter. One of the first attributes to life is happiness we transmit to our young by the way we think and act. Born from love and appreciation, not from possession of possessions, happiness regulates our emotions that in turn release substances from our ductless glands. They run through our blood into our heart, like a steady note, and then over, above, around, and between this keynote undulate further waves combined in a harmonious chord that governs mind and emotion. It helps expand our awareness to leap through time and space.

Gestation varies according to the incarnation, four to five months being the average. The egg is always under observation. We communicate with the developing child once the third principle called the Higher Mind has entered the embryo, which, unlike yourselves, arrives well before birth. The returning ancestor chooses the time of breaking through the egg. Then, gathering in expectation, we stand chanting and watch the child with no umbilical cord emerge through the filmy shell to take its first breath.

In that moment, the Higher Mind, the Higher Self (already in the Keresch foetus) , receives the imprint of our solar system and beyond. We call this aspect of man's composition the Bridge. It joins the physical to the eternal. The Bridge is the super-conscious faculty that threads us to Origin and our spirit, the Immortal *Flame*. In your world, birth is a traumatic experience obliterating memory, and the infant, unlike us, only receives its Higher Mind with its first breath, but like us in that moment instantly absorbs the influences of your the local star map.

---

*Pause again and give yourself time to digest these three principles: the Spark of Life, the material Lower Mind and the inspirational Higher Mind, the principle that we, the Keresch, call the Bridge.*

## CHAPTER 3. JOURNEY THROUGH MYTH AND THE STARS

How can I describe the journey? Take it as an imaginative expedition. Mysteriously drawn from one state into another incarnation on Earth, you pass as a conscious being through the cool eye, the lens of your sun and on through the portals of planets in your solar system, being imprinted on the way by their qualities and astronomical relationships to one another. Each of the astrological signs is an ideogram with a wealth of meanings, a web of energy holding the blueprint, not of your spirit, but the pattern into which you have been drawn. If aware, it is the pattern you have chosen for yourself.

Through your journey, you absorb and carry the resonance of the sun, the planets, and the stars within the very marrow of your bones in a star map you can use or be used by. Stars and planets are vortices. They release more energy into your universe than they receive. Your planets, like beacons, emit specific signals that you translate into astrological qualities.

Your moon is another matter. Should you search deep amongst your ancient myths you will find tales of it having had a gentle people and a high civilisation bombarded into oblivion. Today, pyramids and strange constructions have been photographed on both sides of the moon. With this in mind it is interesting and perhaps not so strange that the Egyptians placed their underworld of judgment and Osiris (god of the afterlife) on the dark side of the moon. The pernicious control of the Anunnaki/Babylonian priesthood continues in an astronomical calendar of the 4th century AD: Romans should ask for assistance from, or have conversation with a man of power when the moon is in Taurus, Leo, Scorpio, or Aquarius.

Over millions of years, from a far-flung galaxy of sources, many races have been seeded, grown, and disappeared on Earth where different kinds of interdimensional beings came to encase souls in evolving vehicles of flesh and blood. In this activity they used, and still use, the moon as a way station for cosmic travellers and their embryonic human baggage to be developed on your unique planet Earth. It was viewed as a piece of prime real estate created in a universe of free will that, by definition, permits conflict. We have always disliked your moon, knowing how it has been a base for controlling your psyche and the energy of your ley lines. Its white face both inspires poets and triggers lunatics. Extraterrestrials have long conducted human experiments there, more to their advantage than yours. However, the electromagnetism of the moon essentially influences the rhythms of tides, form, and growth on Earth.

The Zodiac is a mathematical construct placed on the sky as a circle divided into sections in which the constellations, your sun, and planets can be related in geometric forms (triangle, square, opposition, and others). The divisions are both mathematically commensurate with a circle, and the mystic significance of numbers.

The relationships of planets in the 12 sections of your Zodiac carry the resonance from the geometrics of their waveforms, the vibrations confined and carried within the shapes and pattern formed by their positions to each other. In the same way as a string's vibrations and harmonic frequencies (wave forms) depend on its length, so the geometric combinations in the horoscope indicate their influence. These are expressed in terms of astrological qualities reflected in your human, physical, and psychological constitution. Picture the Zodiac as a circular, tight membrane transmitting the vibrations, the rhythms of celestial orbs in their changing geometric relationships through the seemingly rotating heavens above your Earth. Put in other words, if space defines matter and matter is composed of vibrations, the spatial, geometric designs defined by astronomical relationships can be compared to the harmonic frequencies, the melodies of vibrating strings that vary in sound according to the patterns of their relationships. Changing the geometry changes the vibrations.

Heavenly music has many keys, often recalled by the beguiling songs of Orpheus' mythic harp that kept harmony when chaos was about to break. If astrology be viewed in terms of waveform and its various resonances, in the words of your experts, quantum physics is often no less inconsistent or paradoxical than mysticism. Exact prediction is impossible, leaving mathematics to divine the high probabilities of any theory.

I return to your first breath containing prana (called Qi by the Chinese) , the essence of inhaled air. At the moment you take your first breath, the imprint of the sentient orbs in your Zodiac is etched on your entire personality, qualifying all the subtle factors entrenched in your being. It is like a blueprint but not a definitive, unyielding pattern beyond change. Among your Greek myths is the story of Orpheus and the miraculous harp (or lyre) given to him by his father Apollo, the half- brother of Hermes, and inventor of the instrument. Orpheus lost his young wife Eurydice when, bitten by a snake, she died and fell into the underworld ruled by Hades and his queen, Persephone. Orpheus went to find his lost love.

So enchanting was the music played on his lyre that he was allowed to fetch Eurydice and take her up from Hades, providing he never looked back to see if she were following him. He did, and, for the second time, lost his beloved.

Back on Earth, a heartbroken Orpheus turned from women to find solace with young boys. It provoked the wild wrath of the Thracian women in his homeland.

They tore him limb from limb in a Dionysian rite, signifying the untamed passions that Orpheus' lyre had been unable to counteract. In the Greek Mysteries, the myth refers to the unrestrained violence of our lower nature, that once tamed, transforms Dionysius into Bacchus, guardian of our irrational instincts. The Muses, powers of inspiration, gathered up his remains and buried them, echoing the myth of Osiris whose dismembered body was retrieved (apart from the penis, although in the most ancient texts this was not explicit) in a metaphor of reconstituting a decimated teaching. Conversely, Orpheus descended into the underworld to stay with Eurydice for eternity, and Zeus, to hold unchallenged authority, cast the wondrous lyre into the sky. Although many strong  metaphors  here are never complete, they indicate connections with the various constituents of your psyche. They describe how the higher consciousness becomes entrapped in the lower states, while a disgruntled Zeus, a god-creator, throws the harp sustaining harmony and balance up to its origin in the starry heavens. However there is a tale behind the myth.

Once was a time when from beyond our universe of free will, there entered magnificent beings. They seeded a unique race that formed sentient, singing, and turning orbs with opened crown chakras that released Light emitted as sound in great cosmic symphonies of galaxies where suns and planets formed orchestras communicating in the harmony of the spheres. It brought peace for 4 million years. And then they departed to reside, singing, in the space between universes. There they wait, having transmitted to Homo sapiens music, that not only separated Darkness from Light, but also kept balance between the two. Its range tamed beasts and inspired our Higher Minds.

The cosmic moment has come for us to play and sing them back into our world. Such is already here in the now of our future. The sounds of Orpheus' lyre resonate, vibrating in a harmony specific to humankind, and somehow the memory of this music is sensed across time and space as if by an ear going deaf. You have to unblock your hearing and sing again louder than Zeus' anger! Your poet Shelley (1792-1822), versed in esoteric teachings, wrote in memory:

> *. . . What wondrous sound is that, mournful and faint, . . .*
> *It is the wandering voice of Orpheus' lyre*
> *. . . The waning sound, scattering it like*
> *dew upon the startled sense.*

However, the depressing fate of Orpheus and Eurydice's eternity in the underworld is amended in other teachings. These describe the contest between the forces of Light and the forces of Darkness, penetrated by the presence of an awakened awareness. This classic myth touches on the themes of twin souls separated by the deathly bite of the serpent which could also be the telluric forces bringing souls back into earthly reincarnation, causing the descent of Eurydice (with her higher consciousness) into a lower density, leaving a bereft Orpheus to mourn her loss.

Behind this layered and timeless story stands the most ancient remembrance of soul-seeds coming from Origin through the constellation of Lyra to Earth, before it was attacked and contaminated by Galactic species, resolute in meddling with the psychic and physical aspects of human incarnation.

Having had a hand in your genetic fabric, they still claim their right to rule you. From this came the scenario of ascent when souls leaving Earth pass through your planets and sun, they proceed to the Lyra constellation for purification. It is called the Harvesting of souls who become fodder for the universe's energy.

It could well be true for humans if they betray their inner being. In other words, it is the separation of the wheat from the chaff. One of your more controversial gurus, Gurdjieff, an excellent spiritual trickster, taught that sleepwalkers in your world were no more than moon food. How good it is to read the epitaph on an ancient Greek tomb commemorating an obviously fine navigator who proclaims:

*Do not mourn for me for I am gone behind the moon and beyond the stars to Apollo's gardens of the sun.*

Whenever I watch a birth on our planet I am struck by wonder. At the top end of the cave, in a narrowing alcove, stands a shimmering, nearly transparent egg, revealing the shadowy, lightly pulsating form of the young child curled in a circle about to unfurl. Priests chant, and we watch from behind a protective magnetic shield surrounding the area.

Mantra is far beyond the repetition of a word or vowel to calm the mind into a state of deep meditation. Incantation depends on choosing the correct note, its pitch (the eastern scale with its minute divisions of sound is more accurate than the European), and volume, directed to a specific aim or person. The physical body and its different subtle components each have their signature note, colour and vowel, but, unless applied with expertise, mantra can be dangerous. It's a matter of discovering the connection between sound and thought. In India today they still intone the sacred mantra *AUM (OM)* with the five separate sounds of: *A, U, M,* plus the nasalization and the resonance of the whole word. Five, the pentagram, is also the number of Man.

Accompanied by rolling incantations, the child about to be born breaks the skin of the egg and slowly steps out into the chamber. The magnetic shield that gave the egg an ideal environment is withdrawn and the priests come forward to sprinkle the returned ancestor with magnetized water, chanting together with us: "May the Flames of Origin protect, bless and guide you in all timelines and densities of your multiple incarnations."

We proceed with helping hands to clothe the reborn in white cloaks, and carried on flower-bedecked chairs to sleek, fish-shaped vehicles, we fly them home soundlessly across the land. All our means of transport are virtual extensions of us. Within their sensitive material, they hold a pattern mirroring our DNA, and react immediately to our commands.

Once in the house, our newly reincarnated ancestor takes food in a ritual meal from plates and bowls of precious metals, as well as utensils made with the Japanese aesthetic perfection called *shibumi*. Seated around low tables laden with a banquet, we give praise in word and song before devouring the feast. We prefer to eat low and stand high.

In your world at present, your physicians of the mind and body are unable to distinguish the different densities of energy housed within the body, other than in electrical patterns and auras of Kirlian photography. They think of human consciousness as being divided into categories and functions according to their schools of observations. Beyond the obvious physical brain, the definition of the mind still causes disagreement. In general, it is taken to be like a switchboard relaying various grades of consciousness including clairvoyance.

Where, you might say, is the ghost inside the machine? Does it exist at all? Are we no more than a living chemical laboratory generating thought patterns from a biological organ called the brain? The Keresch have no need for such questions. At birth we have coordinated bodies equivalent to a child of six; we know that we are spirit working within a material vehicle. Speech is easy. We have learnt it in the egg from our cellular memory.

Most Earthlings claiming to remember long consecutive tracts of past lives are deluded by imagination, unless they come from incarnations with a highly-developed awareness. This is often due to an advantageous genetic blueprint strengthened through conscious self-chosen reincarnations found, among others, in some of your high Buddhists. They know the workings of the mind and its projections. Recall is based on your alertness and attention at the time of an event. The more aware you have been, the clearer are your multi- faceted memories that, like strands, plait together your many lives. At this time, we find it is better to incarnate in the body of a genetically mixed Earthling and keep our true identity undercover to avoid difficulties with your authorities. We learnt this by experience. Our repeated intrusion from outside, we decided, would be unproductive. Humanity must stand on its own feet before we openly come to advise. Over half a century ago, an American president had the loaded choice between accepting Galactic help or being coerced into making a pact with Aliens offering technology for war and commerce. The option was there, and the result is yours to cope with. Meantime, in between times, those of us incarnating in your bodies prepare the way for the future. Keep in your heart that in all the diversity of the universe, no man is an island unto himself.

The Creator of your universe knows only Unity. When its infinite energy cascades down condensing into points of awareness and consciousness in the multidimensional universe, the prime points of Logos divide further into denser Logoi. Each has its own central sun, and each has a fused group consciousness of architects in their own spheres manifesting their designs further projected through planetary systems. Each orb (with its higher and lower vibrational surroundings) is a minor Logos radiating its ruling intelligence. The sun in any planetary formation is the most important factor, and a veritable star gate into the wider surrounding universe. All Logoi and their progressively dense sub-Logoi give birth to a variety of architects differentiated in their descent from Unity, and in this differentiation they have seeded a diversity of creatures and extraterrestrials. Not all creators are the same as yours. Their lineage differs; some are compatible, others are not.

At this point let me mention a certain type of human brought into incarnation on your planet. Known as Children of the Sun, they were discreetly protected by certain extraterrestrials more than often connected to the Anunnaki and their genetic programmes. However, there were a limited number of other Children of the Sun, and when not of the Anunnaki's elite illuminati bloodlines, they have a lineage of Light bestowed by other 'fashioners' of your humankind. Your complex and complicated story is a jigsaw puzzle not yet fully told or understood. Rather, remember how Earth's polarity gives two sides to every coin. Polarity offers difference, and difference offers choice to exercise free will, even if debaters claim free will is an illusion, merely appearing free due to the choices being wide enough to hide the limitations! This is not true, for we live in a universe of free will. It is only our ability to choose that has been impaired. In what is known to you as Eden, polarity was split into the duality of good and evil that spiced the apple offered by the snake of wisdom, and regardless of affiliations to Darkness or Light, the apple held the gift of choice so frequently encountered in your ancient sagas such as Orpheus in his wanderings, and other mythical heroes coping with adversity.

---

*Again interrupt your reading and give yourself time to open your imagination to Astrology, Mantra, and Incarnation. Expand your six senses to create your own picture of the words you read and enjoy the result without burdening your intellect with the how.*

*Book of Urizen*

*Eternity shudder'd when they saw,*
*Man begetting his likeness,*
*On his own Divided Image.*

*William Blake (1757 - 1827)*

*Extract from 'The Sphinx'*

*And did you talk with Thoth, and did you hear*
*the moon-horned Io weep?*
*And know the painted kings who slept beneath the wedge - shaped pyramid?*

*OsscarWilde (1854 — 1900)*

## CHAPTER 4.  EGYPT AND TIMES PAST

A long time ago, in the age of a different climate, the north of Africa had soft, warm air. Long grass and trees covered the semi-tropical land. The men of that epoch took the great Nile of Egypt as the earthly counterpart to the celestial waters of the Milky Way. In the past, the river ran much closer to the pyramids passing wide and slow to its swampy delta. In this kingdom of magic and science its lords built edifices of stone, meticulously oriented to the cardinal points of Earth, and in alignment with specific stars in the map of heaven. In the beginning the people were free. They chanted in a workforce of up to 20,000 men building sacred edifices under the guidance of master builders from the motherland of Atlantis. Regardless of texts, kept or lost, the people passed on tales of wonder to their grandchildren, until that world drowned in floodwaters, and left you with only dim memories of the past.

Turn back the pattern of the skies 36,000 years ago to the Spring Equinox. At dawn you will see the eroded lion-bodied Sphinx in straight alignment to its stellar counterpart in the constellation of Leo. Ponder at the mathematics of astronomy that marked so well the wheeling of the Zodiac. Who is to say this star-pointer, this static eye in spiralled time, together with the pyramids, are not monuments commemorating an epoch of so-called gods mingling with you in a forgotten world lost to your recall? We, the Keresch, when on Earth with the Master Builders, helped them levitate stone with our knowledge of vibration. Those with us knew how to lighten mass by altering its structure to resonate at a higher frequency.

We changed its density and the use of sound was part of the equation. The pyramid, said the Galactic architects working with terrestrial initiates, was a magnet for cosmic and telluric energy. If you are content to believe that men bashed rock with metal chisels, and deny the possibility of ancient power tools as well as the technology of changing the molecular density of stone, Then Egypt's monuments will remain an enigma wrapped up in a mystery.

They knew that gravity was a force transmitted down into the pyramid, like a waterfall of star radiance precipitated from the seas of space. The very shape of the pyramid pulled in cosmic energies in a vortex to fill its form where it was adjusted to the human constitution. It was a place for initiates to harmonize their brainwaves with the resonance from the heartbeat of the world, Gaia's throbbing pulse.

On the material level, the pyramids acted as transformers and storage mechanisms of energy, not without danger and mishaps, part of a cautionary tale I barely touch upon in this account. In your mind, come and sit with me in a granite chamber of your own imaginary pyramid built over underground water that augments its electromagnetic power.

In meditation, learn to adjust your brain to the low frequencies moving between the Earth's crust and the ionosphere, frequencies known to you as the Schumann resonance. It can coordinate the pulses of your internal organs to be in tune with the external rhythms permeating all life on your planet. You will slip into altered states, a process made easier within the pyramid's granite walls that amplify your mental and emotional condition. It affects the environment beyond yourselves; it touches the equilibrium of Earth itself. The King's chamber of the great pyramid resonates like a bell to open the heart chakra, the positive charge of the granite being balanced by the negative charge of the outer limestone casing and an alternative charge repeated at the bottom corners of each adjoining side of the pyramid.

For the masses accustomed to wonder at the powers of nature and the night sky, the pyramids were thrones for sky-gods descending to Earth or for the initiation of their hereditary representatives, the god kings of so many cultures. The mythic mind of Cro-Magnon man easily accepted interdimensional humans as deities. Had the intruders always been people of wisdom, man on Earth might have developed faster and become more balanced. Much is forgotten in connection with genetic monitoring by other Galactics who entered into the experiment with the   aim of quickening the evolution of early Earth man, rather than turning him into their slave.

But when the conspiracy of power-driven aliens interfered with human development, there came secrets, lies, false agendas, and control of your fractured psyches, brought low before and after the destruction of Atlantean civilisation.

Teachings known in Atlantis were taken to Egypt and taught in the Mystery Schools, closed about 3,500 years ago after the onset of the Kali Yuga, the age of Darkness, said by some of your Vedic sages to have begun in 3102 BC according to your Julian calendar. It was foretold that this age would be ruled by an influx of beings predisposed to instilling the fear and ignorance, the degeneration and corruption we have always tried to deflect. Today only vestiges of the Mystery Schools have survived, although a certain very secret one still exists. They were closed, hoping to safeguard information that could be used for either destructive or creative purposes, depending on the priests' predilection. So much of Egypt's knowledge came from the migrating peoples of Atlantis. It is fragmented in your modern world, with odd pockets of material evidence, and a few scripts and glyphs found in strange places.

Fly with the eye of a hawk and look down on gigantic monoliths and fallen temples in the Middle East. Glide high over the Himalayan snows guarding libraries in hidden monasteries. Wing south and hover over the Bermuda Triangle with its submerged pyramids, and decipher its anomalies of distortion on time and matter. Swoop over the entangled jungles of Mesoamerica, its deserted temples echoing an Atlantean connection with architecture built to awaken man and to hold the secrets of his soul. But perhaps you forget or overlook the Mesoamerican cult of terrible human sacrifice on reeking altars to appease dark gods. In this area of the world, the Mayan culture was devoted to material intelligence, especially mathematics. You may well recall the violent, blood-splattered tale of creation told in the Popol Vuh. It describes in symbolic terms the creation of man and the disruptions in your planetary system, the latter transposed to games in a ball court. In following my myth you will come to understand why their calendar emphasised your year 2012 AD. That year represented the change whereby the influx of a higher vibration could propel, if not all, certainly some, of humanity into an inner evolution. This marked the break from ancient affiliation with sinister powers, known as the Babylonian Conspiracy, surviving and thriving in your cults of devil worship found everywhere, from the Vatican to underground rooms in the New York building of the United Nations.

You of Earth usually interpret your apocalyptic writings as a forecast for future catastrophe, whereas many of these descriptions, accumulated from ancient scripts and presented in your Bible, refer to the final destruction of Atlantis. However, other prophecies do foretell the potential changes for your planet and its peoples. After Atlantis, I incarnated many times in Egypt (the exact number escapes me while I am on your planet).

The most important one leaves me with a memory lit by a white-hot sun striking polished stone, or a starlit night darker than indigo pierced with the golden tip of the greatest pyramid luminous in an immortal glow.

I am the tall 10-year-old, the only spoilt and adored child of the wily Grand Vizier. I have a playmate born on the same day and year as myself in the month of the Spring Equinox. Inseparable, and a perpetual menace to the servants always attempting to keep us out of mischief, when confronted by my parents we assume an expression of unearthly purity and innocence. Of late we have been scuttling off quick as two field mice towards the reflecting pool housing the sacred crocodiles. We plot death! These animals are the receptacles for divine power associated with the god Seth, the underworld, as well as the sun. Crocodiles rise at dawn from the water. Their fat is used to anoint Pharaohs. We know this and creep to the edge of the pool waiting to drop poisoned meat into their stinking mouths. We hate the beasts connected in our teachings with the powers of Water, Earth and Fire. Not sufficiently tutored, we had yet to learn that the crocodile, marked by the constellation of the Fish, a symbol of inundation, is also the prototype for the mythical solar dragon of life related to Saturn. Crocodiles were specially raised for temples not situated by a lake. They lived in temple pools, some used for initiates ordered to jump in, swim to an underwater opening, continue through a tunnel and hopefully come to air in a secret enclosed hall of the temple. These reptiles, insists the faction of the dark priests, devour those with impure souls. One of our playmates, older than ourselves, a laughing youth always delighted to play games with us, had failed his trial and been devoured by these monsters. Quietly chanting an incantation invoking revenge overheard from our chief cook in one of his frequent furies, we throw our hunks of poisoned meat into the teeth of the household crocodiles. We leave them to float pale-belly-up in the water.

An hour later uproar breaks through our domain: hoots from the ervants, roars from the guards, and ululating trills from all the women running in a rush hither and thither between gardeners, porters, sweepers, artisans, washers, and secretaries, all under orders from my enraged father to find us. Two weavers discover us hiding under piles of fresh pleated linen. Dragged by the ears, stifling our squeals, we are tumbled off to confront our distressed parents. Mother is dignified. Father is red with anger.

"Take them to the temple!" he thunders. This time, surrounded by the household crowd reduced to silence, we scream at the top of our young voices. The vividness of this scene still brings me much amusement. The High Priest, a very high priest, a thin man with an unremarkable face illuminated with eyes as clear and pure as rock water, greets us with a stern expression hiding the mirth in his gaze. We have known him since our earliest years of attending celebrations as children of a renowned family. With a disregard for adults and the gravity of the situation, we grin up at him, trying to check the laughter in our throats. The most High Priest, assuming his unquestionable authority, prevents any punishment for our sacrilegious comportment that he decides requires priestly rather than parental discipline. He, for some reason, sees more than meets the eye with the two us of us. This is our entrance into the temple training for the next decade.

My little friend, the daughter of one of my father's concubines, and born on the evening after my birth, accompanies me all the way. We grew up together, first dashing around on our hands and feet (rather than on knees), then walking together with a complicity my mother tells me comes from our association in a previous incarnation. In our early years I pass by the temple, a forest of stone columns upholding arcades of shade, to the adjacent library, the House of Life. There we learn the art of writing, numbers, the necessity of correct protocol, as well as sacred dance, song, and stories of our pantheon.

After puberty we graduate to the outer grades of sacred knowledge. In our training, like my childhood friend, I recall parts of our life working together in Atlantis under traumatic conditions. We also attend the royal school for the courtiers educated with the princes and princesses of the realm.

In the early years, our teachers familiarize us with the temple's hieroglyphics and paintings. Once we can read the obvious, we are tutored to mingle intuition with education and open a stream of associations for interpreting the esoteric meaning behind the visual representation. As the demotic language altered over time, the high priests guarded the phonetic elements of the word, including words with similar sounds but different meaning. It was an intricate association in a three-fold manner of interpretation using sound, words, and their pictorial representation understood through obvious and later occult significance reserved for initiates.

The Egyptians knew the creative quality of sound. The hieroglyphics embalmed the creative agents of the world, revived through the articulation of sound in sacred words expressed in a divine writing from the land lost beneath the Western Seas. I learn to read texts telling of our first and second line of rulers, the gods, and then the companions of Horus, a particular branch of humanity, an ancient and special lineage composed of people with minds in touch with the creative intelligences of the life sustaining sun; an ability traditionally bestowed upon all our Pharaohs because of their bloodline and connection with the ancestors. Their heredity upholds their power and the authority of priests, although I think it is only our great hierophants who transmit how to see through time and space, and apply the laws of magic. Translation into other languages lost the original sound, the hidden keystone that held the powers of creation in a system of sacred etymology. With training we learnt how sound alone could transmit a many-faceted idea in a code handed down through generations of scholars. In many ways we were prisoners of time, locked into a system, with the answers to any imbalance in the environment theoretically found in the formula for its rectification deciphered from the ancient texts first given when the gods descended to Earth.

The laws of an eternal and, for us, unchanging universe nonetheless had a modicum of freedom within their constituents that caused imbalance. Adjustment came by referring back to our accumulated wisdom applied in mathematics, the energy of rites linked to the sun, seasonal change and astronomy. You could say that in Egypt magic of any hue was a science as much as an art.

Nothing, said the savants, whatever it may be, has not been done and inscribed in our temples. All answers were there to be discovered anew. I leave complicated research to our specialised priests and concentrate on learning a casket-full of magic incantation for protection. Oh Egypt, how your Light is eaten by the maggots of the black arts, so often stemming from Ethiopia. The power of the arcane in our teachings had to equate with moral responsibility, seldom an immutable equation. The secret teachings of both Light and Darkness coexisted in our temple, and many were the compromises between the priests unless the polarity was too great, and when I would hear my mentor mumble to himself, "Fanatics exhaust me!"

One symbol can retain a book. Once absorbed it helps me merge with the living presence of our temple, The Enclosure of the KA of Ptah, our god of creation. Repetitive as it is, the time I love most comes with the breaking of dawn. It is then that I sense the temple within myself.

During the thick silence of night on the ramparts of the sacred compound, the time-marker, the sereno, has stood watching the passage of stars. He notes the hours, and at his call, just before the first light, life within the temple's walls awakens. Artisans, bakers, builders, and butchers ready to kill the sacred animals for sacrifice, enter to begin their work. The day's ceremonial offerings are prepared. Some priests place globs of milky frankincense on hot coals. Others make their twice-daily ablutions in the waters of the temple's sacred lake that carry the metaphysical gift of regeneration. Most priests are temple functionaries with hereditary duties and pompous titles. They are administrators with no particular spiritual ambitions. Others indeed teach and study in our House of Life, the temple's vast library, where we start building an inner architecture to house divine wisdom. But the multitude of priests, when not fulfilling functions in rotating shifts throughout the year, return home to continue their profession or trade in a normal family life.

Each day everything must be purified, made ready for the great god Ptah, our divine patron, who sends part of his essence into his statue standing in the inner sanctum, the naos, its nightly seal broken anew each dawn. The sun rises red on the horizon. How close to me still is that piercing cry: "Rise thou great god. Rise thou in peace!" answered by a throng of voices chanting, "Rise thou so beautiful in peace. "Then the soloist again intones in full voice, "Thou with radiant visage that knows no anger ... thou who spreads thy golden dust over the Earth." And my heart responds to this morning chant perpetuated since the birth of our civilization.

Its call pierces through the grey light, out and over the smoke of early fires from the surrounding human settlement. For the dawn ritual of Face to Face, the High Priest lights a candle in the naos. Shadows dance on the vibrant colours of the decorated walls. Sacred objects and chests of treasure glint fleetingly as he breaks opens the wooden doors enclosing the basalt effigy of our deity, ready to leave Darkness for Light at the exact moment when the sun tips above the eastern horizon. Only the Pharaoh and his substitute, the High Priest, can stand face to face before a temple's main god.

The many magnificent ceremonial offerings of food, drink, and flowers, as well as the perfuming and dressing of the god's effigy for processions, are not just rituals appeasing human needs. Shared by the gods when they appeared on Earth, they are reverences to that divine essence attracted to and embodied in the living statue through secret rites.

It is the same essence that envelops everything on this Earth and sustains the movement of the heavens. We give praise to an all-encompassing divinity of creation. Oh Egypt! Your temples hold magic and many lost mysteries. I know the towering pillared spaces built on mathematical proportions of the geometry underlying the form of the world we live in. They incorporate sacred proportions, which extend in the sequence of numbers generating the cosmic pattern of life, stamped in shells and the ram's curling horns. The harmony of heaven is mirrored and anchored in mute stone. Beware! Our temple lives with the power that midnight's dark thieving priests covet in order to control the Pharaoh and his kingdom.

I learn the sciences of medicine and music, as well as alchemy in the context of transforming oneself more than metals. I find joy in dance, taking part in sumptuous annual pageants that portray the lives of our main deities. I am taught the basics of astronomy and geometry, but higher calculations are reserved for the more gifted; in other terms, we women were discriminated against in these teachings. Nonetheless, in my group we outnumber the men in the art of projecting our awareness beyond physical sight by awakening our pineal gland. Its vision is unimpeded by time and space. The altered sense of sight projects itself to objects hidden from the physical eye in distant places and events, past, present, or future of this world.

Other realms come to view in an extended sight via the third eye. It is even better when the shadow body leaves its physical counterpart, although always joined by a silver cord extending from the crown, or the forehead chakra. Mastering the sacred arts and sciences needs time. When we take the extract of the blue water lily under careful supervision it changes our perceptions, and we see, hear, and talk with strange beings of mixed shapes, with guardian animal spirits, and with radiant people living in ethereal light, and at times a false light that can trap us.

The human constitution, physical and psychic, is a combination of principles encased in sheathes of different densities. Like all orbs, from atoms to planets, suns and galaxies, your visible body is surrounded by an invisible aura. This outer sheath encases the physical form in which other sheaths of subtle densities house different principles and functions. All sheaths are eventually released in the return to our Immortal Flame abiding in Origin.

Some more than others have inherited the gift of consciously slipping out of their body, and clothed in a finer form, housing what we in Egypt call the KA, or the dark blue shadow-self, they pass into other realms. The advanced initiate also uses the most rarefied component of his being called the BA, the intelligence concomitant with Light. The BA, with its own subtle body, is the Bridge to Origin. We portray it as the hawk carrying this part of your consciousness back to its source. It is the highest aspect of our incarnated being and, once the initiate is awoken, he or she can observe and direct their KA in dreams. Once in the body of their BA *(the Higher Self)*, they can receive and send images in clairvoyance. They can also communicate telepathically. They are healers, and, as hierophants, can project a holistic image of themselves. I have already mentioned the KA and the BA, the principles of the Lower and Higher Mind, when they enter the growing foetus in the birth chambers of my home planet.

Come the time as young initiates in the outer grades, the two of us, on the advent of sexuality, behave disgracefully, taking wicked pleasure in partly seducing over-serious and grave youths who wished to dedicate their lives to the purity of abstinence. This practice was supposedly thought to grant greater metaphysical power, an idea by no means imposed in our training, and unlike other nations of our time, when places of worship often supported holy prostitutes, any form of sexual activity is forbidden within our temple compound. Regardless of our flirtations having taken place in the countryside, the most High Priest is very upset.

Lessons in our internal alchemy, he reprimands us, have in this respect failed miserably.

"What are you doing? You have humiliated young people of good intent.

"You in whom I have tried to instill a modicum of ethical behaviour and responsibility essential for initiates! It is no excuse telling me your play with seduction took place beyond the temple area. Your intentions were wrong. Need I remind you of the consequences that will beset you from your own conscience in time to come? Maybe even sooner than you think."

He turns abruptly leaving us in searing remorse. Predictably, that time comes only too soon and I receive a merited humiliation from a person remembered to this day, but with whom, in this life, I have made my peace.

In Egypt, all knowledge is taught on different levels demanding grades often dangerous to pass. My time has come. We, the initiates, have to ritually endure physical tests, often disastrous when put in the wrong hands. I experience the rumblings of fear due to certain adepts using the merciless power of the Left Hand path to pervert the trials. Death during a test could eliminate a potentially powerful troublemaker. Over time, rituals no longer appropriate for changing cultures have been altered. In your present stage of development, it is not always necessary for you to physically undergo certain trials or walk for miles to a holy place. At present it can be done in your more evolved imagination. The memory of an actual event or an imaginary one is registered in the same areaof the brain.

In the past you might have lost your life in unnecessarily perilous initiations, but, at present, your psychic constitution is damaged and manipulated by your education and propaganda. The result is achieved through the mind rather than the body.

Initiation was, and is, a control system as much as any. Today, people aware of their inner core have the possibility of lifting their own and the vibrational field around them by the act of practicing an enlightened ethic, not just complying intellectually to a set of rules. The rituals of initiation played their role in giving humans a sense of belonging and achievement still sought today. Rites remain important for developing teenagers before true maturity brings self-confidence and assessment of one's capabilities and failings without some guru putting one to trial.

At my graduation by trial in the pool of crocodiles, when told to dive in I refuse. I turn my back without even glancing at the priest giving orders. "Fools!" I think. "I see you, dark priests hiding behind pillars, have me in your sights. You know I will be trouble. No! I will not play your game of death."

Since we are on the cusp of the Kali Yuga, those of the Left Hand path fight the Light and infiltrate our ceremonies in the mystery schools. Perhaps my decision saved my life, although it simultaneously exposed my lack of confidence in the most High Priest's protection, for which I promptly and humbly apologise. He smiles and says, "You possibly showed a grain of common sense subsequently adopted by your friend and I will not prevent either of you from further tuition. It would disrupt the healing of your past relationship in Atlantis". He adds, "Also, an increased intelligence and greater psychic powers are not necessarily an indication of a greater beatitude, unless you practice what you have learnt. Apply everything you have learnt, and that will be the level of your initiation."

Only at this time did my mentor explain the co-existence in our temple of teachings from the Light as well as from the Shadow. In the paradox of power, the priests of both sides have, throughout time, worked side by side keeping equilibrium, a give and take, rather than a static balance, unless there be too many fanatics insisting on a victory without any compromise.

"Save me from those exhausting extremists!" he would repeatedly mumble to himself, but still loud enough for us to hear and smile.

When the right time comes, the most High Priest, he whose entire being issues a simplicity encasing his extraordinary but seldom demonstrated power, prepares me for the rite of second birth. I once more feel a fleeting fear. It is an essential step in my awakening. It can be unsuccessful if the initiate, having left his mortal body for at least a day and night, is lost or overpowered on entering both lower and higher realms to observe and speak with the great deities of Nature, demonic or angelic, and to stand before the beings we regard as our gods. The days of preparation include cleansing on every level. All hair on my body is removed. I break the fast with liquid herbal essences, taken before and after reciting long tracts of incantations cobwebbed with time. Furthermore, through the music of drum, harp, and flute, my detachment from the material world strengthens.

In the heightened awareness of semi-trance I am helped into not a stone, but a gilded cask of sweet, pungent wood. There is no lid. My body wrapped lightly in a fine white cloth, and is carried in the cask to some secret place I know not where. Through breath and concentration, I rise out of my body, and, without looking back, I move towards two beings standing in a rainbow of colours.

I am taken, guided, flying between them to pass in the blink of an eye through veils of different textures until I stand, my feet not quite on the ground, surrounded by breathless beauty filled with strange and sublime music. I enter the core of those sounds and, feeling large as a cosmic god, watch stars being born from placentas of mist. No more will I say, other than from lightness I am sucked into the heaviness. From brightness I descend into terrifying caverns of gloom.

I come face to face with Anubis, the sly dog-faced guardian of the Egyptian netherworld. He demands my heart if I am to pass into as well as return from this underworld. I refuse. "My heart is the seat of my *BA*," I reply.

"It is my own. I am not yet dead and stand no judgment now. You   must    let me pass." Straight after repeating a magic text for Light, "Come to me good. You who are entirely good, You whom no magic can enchant…" I walk on to stand before the shadow-self, the dark blue KA of the great Lord Osiris, god of death and rebirth. He abides in a higher realm of Light. It is his shadow-self that when I die will weigh my merit against a feather on the scales of justice. In images depicting the  myth of Osiris' life when on Earth, I see his body, symbolic of his knowledge, dismembered, lost, and partly re-found in futures I will come to know. Passing through these scenes I exit from this psychic imprint of Egypt, the group agreement of a cultural reality perpetuated by our minds over eons, and I see the Sphinx, our guardian, looking out from a pallid and waning moon.

We in Egypt have kept much but cannot retain our ancient wisdom. I watch our land pass through a descending cycle. I see our knowledge degenerate from its  origin. Yet it embalms ancient sciences and metaphysical complexities in myths protecting information that will be deciphered again.  Never   without   danger.  Power itself is neutral. It can to be used for destruction or creation in relation to your intention. Then, in a flash from thousands of years in the future, comes a vision of the pyramids. Reconstituted, tipped in gold and encased in crystal, they release  the song of the Earth in contact with the heavens. They, as well as our earthly Sphinx, rise from islands in a shallow, transparent lake. She you call Gaia is at peace.

As I remain stationary  in  moving  space, I am surrounded by cosmic powers taken human form, along with many beings of man-like countenance: star people, our gods, people of unknown origin, and others in strange conjunctions, as if everything is happening at the same time in the same location. Feeling pain and ecstasy, I observe the distortion of linear perception in a cosmic holograph. Much more I see until the polarity of experiences fades, and, devoid of form, I sense in     the silence with no available word what I am…a presence, a  consciousness  immersed in the thundering silence, the great  untranslatable  state  of  the  All  that is before, during, and after manifestation. To even apprehend it is a presumption. I also sense danger in having no wish to return from this mystic reflection, only a reflection of an ultimate actuality beyond my earthly illusion. Then, seemingly like a stone shattering the surface of an endless lake of mercury, the call of the most High Priest brings me back.

I open my eyes in darkness. My heart beats to explode before fainting as he helps me out of the casket. The circumstance for me to remain in that awareness will not arrive until I complete my earthly experiences and many more in the higher realms. Recalled to Earth, reborn in the occult sense, I am still bound by time and the incarnations I choose as a means to gain experience, adjustment, and knowledge, rather than a state entered into in the name of punishment. I had also vaguely sensed perplexing conditions about time and consciousness experienced during my rebirth. Perhaps it held the seeds of change beyond habit, beyond perpetuating form and content, to always exist limited in the imprint of inviolate archetypes. My incomplete understanding of my journey into the double vortex of simultaneous expansion and contraction leaves me feeling closer than ever to my mentor. However, our obvious spiritual bond by no means lightens or enlightens the way his wife treats me. A goose of a woman, she is always on guard, her old wings flapping and beak open in squawks on anyone wishing to approach her husband. She hates me. My feeling is one of exhausting frustration. She is so stupid. The most High Priest likes her. "She looks after me!" he says in childlike simplicity. Silly or not, this woman makes my life a misery.

Soon after accepting a marriage my parents offer me, my time in the temple is reduced to periods of study in the House of Life and participation in pageants and cyclic ceremonies. I place no restriction on my practice of healing and foresight applied in my home sanctuary. Before departure at the end of that year's term in the temple, the most High Priest, my deeply respected mentor, calls me into a curtained room behind the inner sanctum. He with the side plait falling from a shaved head, he with white sandals and jewel-studded collar covering his shoulders, knows how to embed or retrieve memories. Likewise, the Dark Ones could also implant false images as do covert organizations today using artificial intelligence. Led to a thonged bed, he, the master of storms, the alchemist, the unseen healer, he who can project not only his awareness but also his holographic form for anyone to see, inserts a long spiralled needle of monatomic gold into points below my ankles. "This," he explains, "will etch the memory of this life within your coming incarnations. We will meet. You will remember and be reintroduced anew to the ancient wisdom you have known over so many lifetimes. I have already taught you how to, as it were, look into the mirror and see your future self.

He, from the Galactic race of Ancient Beings, the Watchers, also known as the Guardians and Observers, the Wise Ones, who in their silence always knew the plans of the Anunnaki in Atlantis, in Egypt, Middle America, in the Middle East and India, returns as a high priest of the mysteries on a Greek Isle. Long centuries later from our secret union I bear his son, a child of mixed heritage who marks your world by taking part in a strategy to outwit the Dark Hierarchies that dominate this world. Like others, I know only a small part of this great perspective, a part of the process that involves breaking and re-assembling the patterns of your mind and body.

Knowing that my further encounter with this hidden master awaits deep in another epoch, I must recall his teachings as a measure of truth for certain people in the future brilliant with false prophets, half-truths, and uncertainty. On restricting my time in the temple, my childhood friend follows suit. I cover her identity to be revealed later in this myth. We both marry well, and, on the death of my spouse, I continue to administer our house and lands. The dark is gaining power in stealing the secrets of sacred science. The priests are fighting, each contingent plotting for its own supremacy. They want the power of the pyramids.

In the beginning, the great hierophants who fostered the Atlanteans built pyramids to harness Nature's energy and applied geometry to architecture for mathematical, geophysical, and psycho/spiritual essentials. If you recall the principle told in your fairy tales of the genie caught in the bottle, enslaved to his master, and if let loose wreaks havoc, then bring into the scenario the archetypal Merlin Mind that when incarnating in human form can tame the Elements. Each Element, seen in mystic terms as the building blocks for life and manifestation, gives birth and power to wondrous shape-shifters known as elementals. They are without human conscience. Each category can only exist and participate in its particular essence of Earth, Air, Fire or Water, and if trapped within a material confine, unless ruled by a magus, they are dangerous. The vibrations of specific sound and rhythm when related to the four elements, release their powers used for good or evil purposes.

During a certain period, the Dark Masters usurped the place of the White Hierophants, and took control of the elementals they used to harness Nature's forces. In the last conflict between the two opposing groups of savants an explosion in the Great Pyramid broke vibrational barriers controlling these unruly entities, that, if enchained without a master, exist as vampires. They suck energy from anyone who has the misfortune to make contact with them. To exorcise their presence requires immense knowledge and power. Just as the Egyptians chained the *KA* of an important person to his mummy knowing it would preserve the existence of the *KA* as a guardian of the embalmed body and tomb, elementals were similarly confined to the body of the pyramid. Since their release would entail their disintegration back into the element from which they came, they do their utmost to resist any form of banishment. The design of the Great Pyramid can be seen as a partial analogy to the composition of a human being with places for the heart, brain, and further invisible components of your make up.

I wish to stay aloof, minding my own business, holding my inner teachings to myself, unless I speak with the most High Priest, his body now slowly fading into frailty and age. Together with overseeing my vast property and its people, I keep in touch with my childhood playmate, and, being childless, I take great interest in her twin sons.

---

*Rest and remember these teachings of the High Priest. Find your own memories of Egypt, its reverberation passed on through countless people returning in groups corresponding to the times when they incarnated there together. Was this through free choice?*

*Then when the moon is full, the dark, dog-headed Anubis*
*will howl for the souls he could not devour.*

*Extract from a protective Egyptian incantation.*

*Les Formateurs*

*We came with Heaven's quick Spark of Life*
*And flame to light the crystal air And so*
*illuminate your sight*
*And keep your strangely-fractured psyches*
*From living in a moonless night.*
*So let discarnate Spirit fuse*
*With heart and mind and timeless muse*
*Who keeping count of all yourselves Knows*
*mirrored mansions where they dwell*
*And guards your many secrets well.*

*Keresch chant for Earthlings.*

## CHAPTER 5.  KERESCH. ANUNNAKI. AVATARS

How, you might ask, do we move through time and space? I would answer: similarly to the way you send and receive in telepathy.

In the words of your great physicist Max Planck, mind is the matrix of matter. We train to project our consciousness to any place we choose, in what you would term inner and outer space. Through breath, intention, practice, and will enhanced by a subtle nervous energy, our ability is increased to transfer an interior idea into an outer form. Much is based on the laws of correspondence, meaning compatibility between resonance (the prolongation of sound), vibration (the oscillation of an electromagnetic wave), and velocity. On another level it is the application of sound intertwined with the specific wavelengths of thought.

In our brain, unlike yours, we have a membrane, an organ of perception wrapped across our frontal lobes that have hardly any division between them. We process information from a very wide scale of frequencies. Just as dolphins have a structure in their paralimbic cortex which decodes with extreme rapidity sound relayed from a melon-like lens of fatty tissue above their blowhole, this ear-eye both sends and receives ultra- low sound waves, and similar to our membrane, it helps them make contact with other realities. The dolphins on your planet have their own tale to tell, a lovely history stemming from the stars. Think of them as swimming in shining shoals from the Waters of Space to glide, turn, and leap into your seas. They, like yourselves, have been brought from elsewhere to develop on your unique orb.

The brain is a physiological structure. The mind is energy within that structure and can have awareness beyond its physical seat. The mind can record and attune itself like an adapter to receive or send information from other levels of consciousness, usually transmitted on a lower harmonic. High amplitude brainwaves produced in states of quietude also open you to an extended awareness. The gamma frequencies enable contact with evolved entities, often both seen and heard.

For all your current explanations of altered states being related to brain chemistry, consciousness should never be equated with electrical engineering or chipped artificial intelligence. Consciousness, co-existent with primal substance, is an aspect of *Origin* transcending energy, as you know it. For the alchemists, consciousness is the primal material.

As you must have gathered, we have come and gone on Earth for eons, influencing your arts in many ways. Conversely, any science coming from outer space and hardly tainted by cultural beliefs, when brought to your planet, is restricted and often forbidden by your religious and political doctrines determined to control your minds. Give thanks for the shooting stars of genius that burst forth, breaking the bonds of your genetic castration in unpredictable ways. Perhaps it is your ability to express strong emotions from ecstasy to heartbreak that we, better than many interdimensional types, can identify with. We, the Keresch, learnt it was often better to incarnate in the body of a genetically-mixed Earthling and keep our true identity under cover to avoid open confrontation with the Anunnaki and their compatriots.

Our incarnations also leave an imprint on the KA and its development as a conscious, living entity. Any change we make in our genome while on Earth also affects the future of humanity.

Work this through and I am sure you will get it, and have a glimpse of the importance of compatible Galactics incarnating here with their long-term view of going beyond their temporary discomfort.

You could call some of us tall. Our height can reach to over eight feet, and our hair, bound for work and war, hangs like a living cloak when at leisure. In meditation it can rise in an aureole around our heads. Our skin ranges from golden to rust and shining onyx black. Our long eyes resemble those seen in the paintings of Cimabue and the later Masaccio of the Italian Quattrocento. Because we incarnated with other Galactics during that period, at present our clan retains a preference for its own style of dress adapted to personal tastes, whereas others, on their first contact with humans in Africa, were so astonished at the beauty of black skin and flashing white teeth bared in laughter, that they later genetically modified their skin tone to please themselves.

Our resemblance to you, when manifesting or landing directly from our craft, is strong enough to let us pass undetected if we are not too tall and remain discreet with as little visibility as possible. Only Earthlings with inner sight would notice the brightness of our aura, accepting in times past that it was the mark of people chosen by their gods. We learnt how to contain its emanations as we adapted to your environment. At first stifling and heavy as lead, it would near crush us on stepping from our ships adjusted to your frequencies for landing. The sooner we adapted to Earth's pressure the better, if only for a limited period.

The union of man and woman, once similar to your ways, evolved into a much deeper and wider connection. Ecstasy is reached in a tantric alchemical blending of mind and emotion, projecting awareness into the universe of embracing, unrestricted joy. Straightforward as that, it makes your sexual problems hopelessly laughable. Your manipulated genetic helix leaves the pleasures of sex like a drug of passing happiness because you have lost the subtle connection to an existence wider than the function of your five, and sometimes six, senses.

Humour is always a relief. It lightens the pretensions dividing holy from profane love propagated by popes and prelates of your Christianity, as well as fanatic Muslims and certain Buddhist sects that forbid their monks, born of woman, never ever        to touch a female.

In the seventeenth century the Italian baroque sculptor, Bernini, in a subversive joke against Catholic doctrine, made a technically astounding statue of St. Theresa in ecstasy.

She lies limp under her flowing nun's habit, head thrown back, lips parted, eyes half closed in orgasmic release, as a young male angel stands over her with a somewhat smug smile on his face, waiting to pierce her with the arrow of love raised to a heavenly playing field. Are you supposed to accept this as a representation of blending with the Holy at its highest level?

Your religious doctrines have long upheld the division between dirty body and clean spirit. Bringing to mind the words of one of your great thinkers, Sir Thomas More, when he remarked in the sixteenth century:

*"Sex and religion are closer to each other than either might prefer."*

How witty that in a Roman church, Bernini's statue epitomising sexual ecstasy is simultaneously a metaphor for unification with Christ ... and why not, if this is the only way diminished humans can find short-term bliss, with their cables to heaven reduced to two strands, severed from their environment of nourishment termed junk DNA?

The twelve-stranded DNA you talk about could just as well be taken as a modern hieroglyph for increasing the capacity of your genes to receive a wider range of subtle data from the twelve segments of your Zodiac.

So much has been divulged about the Anunnaki genetic experimentation that I will not go into the subject other than to say there is Darkness within Light and Light within Darkness. Where there is spin, the spin of any orb, there is polarity necessary for manifestation. According to this principle, your planet has a dangerous degree of polarity causing great friction and the perception of duality, but also it gives rise to an extraordinary variety of species. Over the eons involved with Earth, some of the Anunnaki and their helpers have moved towards the Light, probably concluding that their evolution lay with the mixed-blooded humans.

Awakening is a painful progress similar to the sensations of a frozen limb being resuscitated back to feeling, combined with an influx of unexpected and even previously unknown emotions. It is a complicated and complex situation. You Earthlings, part creation of the Anunnaki, part creation of other Galactics, will be the pupils who surpass their masters. You will, for those who choose, be the means of their illumination. You will, due to your mixed genes, eventually transmit to them what they tried to steal from you. The secret is that they cannot take what they want from you, whereas you can give them what they want when the time comes. When?

Think about it and await your own answer.

Our planet is not a paradise of eternal peace. We know the menace of other races that challenged and disrupted our peace. In defending our way of being we were forced into change. The influence of Fire was too strong in our character. It had to be transmuted.

After the last great battle with the Cysts, we knew how we had overstepped the mark in war. The Council in its silence never forbade us entry and our seats were always there. But although we were informed about the conferences, if not overtly invited, in our pride we never appeared. We were self-expelled, until a woman and a man, sent forth from our Dreamers, preferred to project their appearance rather than incarnate on our planet. The First Born from Origin sent these two beings as Avatars, or, in your Christian terminology, saviours. You claim Jesus the Christ came directly from your God, the Creator. The virgin birth of Jesus of Nazareth was an acceptable explanation for a human said to be an immaculate conception when it was the birth of a particular interdimensional man, sent from Origin and carrying its reflection of Immaculate Consciousness into an earthly body. Christians accept your Jesus of Nazareth as the only son of God: born and crucified. Certain Essenes did not believe this.

The true history of your Jesus will be known one day. Never nailed to the cross, he travelled to the Himalayas, Ireland and further afield. Then, strangely, the forces of Light as much as the Dark Powers decided that he should be taken out of the game. Jesus spoke too much, too soon, about the secret of freedom to the uninitiated. He was dangerous to both sides overridden by zealots who left no room for resolution, hence his departure is better left to mystery. Others claim a surrogate was crucified. For some experts the shroud of Turin bears the imprint of a man crucified circa 64 BC. Known as the Master of Righteousness (a title applied to an office as much as a person), this great Qumran teacher's work was unsettlingly similar to Jesus of Nazareth. Both men were acclaimed Messiahs.

Crucifixion reanimates images of my time with the Cathars. I feel like an Olympic runner bearing the torch of remembrance through the geography of places and lives in your world. Every experience leaves its significance in my being, although this time I only come into your environment for a few years to help safeguard sacred scripts and observe the misplaced strength in your fanatical emotions, so frequently chained in an oath of fidelity to an idea.

We, the Keresch, have never wished to impose our way of being on your planet. It would be useless. We are both at different stages of development on different planets with very different electromagnetic surrounds.

On Earth, the polarity alone makes it extremely difficult for you to master your emotions. We can but bring you information at appropriate times and wait for you, interlinked with your environment, to change. We too have strong emotions and therefore understand your difficulties. Unfortunately, it is not for us to control your excess of feelings, a problem occasionally solved with remarkable love and courage by those of your kind who, often but not always, retreat from normal life in the search for spirituality. We must leave you to find your own ways.

---

*Time to close, and should you wish, supplement the information with your own research, your own ideas about the subjects mentioned.*

*To succeed in the world, it is far more necessary*
*to possess the penetration to discern who is a fool,*
*than to discover who is a clever man.*

*Charles Maurice de Talleyrand 1754-1838*

*Keresch conundrum*

*The results of actions in time, take time and times*
*for their impact to be timely in all times of time itself.*

## CHAPTER 6. THE CATHARS

The theme of emotions and their excesses brings me to my short stay with the Cathars, a somewhat heretical but ostensibly Christian sect. In the first half of the thirteenth century 40,000 of them were tortured, burnt, and killed in the southern territory of Languedoc, France. I tell their story as an epic of spirit. They had little more than a few thousand ministers, and, when persecuted, their strength of conviction and the increasing number of converts undermined both king and pope.

They practiced what they preached, and in charity worked to unite man's body and soul with spirit, the indwelling divinity that they considered had fallen from heaven. They remain in your eyes a partially-enigmatic OR mystic-sect with a core of ancient, suppressed teachings that challenged institutionalized Christianity, its corruption and power, in Rome.

On returning to your world, having done my homework, I arrive, an orphaned young Cathar woman from a congregation in northern Italy. In these diverse communities, each with regional interpretations of their faith, I am accepted as an initiate among initiates due to our unity coming from mystical insight obtained during our rites of purification. We were bound to each other through having become "Sons and Daughters of the Light Mind" (comparable in conventional Christian terms to the Holy Spirit). Each soul was a fragment of this Light, that when united, formed a glowing Unity of Mind. It soldered their communities together, however geographically dispersed they might be.

The wind brings dust, carrying the dry smell of lavender and thyme across the good earth. It is 1240 in your Anno Domini. I come as an observer in yet another crucial period of struggle between the powers of Light and Darkness. Your world's severe polarity is so well shown in the history of the Cathars... and others in a similar position. They hold their beliefs against the fire and sword sent by the pope to exterminate their unorthodox teachings. The Catholic powers are soon aided with the brutal force of a black robed Catalonian priest named Guzman, destined to initiate the iron fist of the inquisition in Languedoc.

He represents the totalitarian authority beloved by the hard-line Anunnaki since their first foot holds on your world. The Catholic Church will later canonize him as Saint Dominique. However, I must add that your contemporary teaching order of Dominicans is doing its best to expurgate the violence of their founder's methods, and the horrors of the inquisition. Although the Cathars were professed Christians, portions of their faith, like so much of esoteric thought, had sailed and footed its way from Atlantis into Egypt, Europe, and on to mid-Asia in the times of migration before the last inundation around 12,000 years ago.

During the journey much was of the ancient mysteries were distorted and increasingly forgotten under the hold of the dark Anunnaki construct. Their intervention on your planet encouraged doctrines of a dualism in which two opposing forces in a managed conflict produce a synthesis that benefits those who have controlled the conflict.

The hidden powers of the Anunnaki (also termed the Babylonian Priesthood) in your world have used these tactics from time immemorial, exemplified in the cosmic combat between the Creator and his chief fallen angel, who the Christians call Lucifer, and who the Cathars call master of your planet. As usual, in a game of feigned retreat and advance, the rulers of this world, in watching the Cathars, permitted them to establish their faith.

They had already used the same tactics in the early Christian Gnostic Church before controlling the results through dividing and ruling, and holding in Rome the keys of the Pope's proclaimed Kingdom on Earth and Heaven.

Without telling the details of the demise of this stubborn sect in Languedoc, I will set the scene by saying the land is rich from trade and boasts a mixed and relatively tolerant culture of Christians, Jews, and Arabs. Plato is studied at the budding

University of Montpellier. The great prince of this large territory fears neither the King of England, France, nor Aragon in Spain. This is an age of violence and fervent emotion. In hatred or devotion only the latter is modified by mores of gallantry exemplified in the search for spiritual perfection found in the stories of questing for the Holy Grail and the eloquent troubadours who sing of ethereal love set in a brutal society.

Often such idealised love is both a gauze masking carnal affiliations, or a sincere desire to unite, through platonic adoration, man's lower nature with his pure soul represented by an ideal woman… so charmingly illustrated in the tapestries of the unicorn, symbol of male eroticism, being tamed by laying its head in the lap of a virgin. If the pen writes of perfection, the sword writes its message in carnage justified in the name of God.

Crusades in the Holy Land are starting to lose their allure with the crown of Jerusalem lost to Islam, and the cost of war is high. Languedoc holds wealth. Its ties to Rome are slack and inefficient. It is time for the pope to instigate a crusade against fellow Christians to gain assets and influence. Furthermore, politically, the King of France also considers the realm of Languedoc too independent. Just as important a number of its great lords, if not already Cathars, protect this clean-cut sect of dissent. Many of its adepts have attained the magic of a presence often more influential than words. Their power over his flock, roars the Pope, has to be wiped out.

Another strength of this deviant group resides in the attraction of a rich inner life and the manipulation of energy. They pray a lot, and in the obligatory Lord's Prayer repeated daily, they replace the daily bread with super-ubstantial bread, coupling an outward simplicity with mysticism. Their ordained priests, the Perfect Ones (more correctly the Completed Ones), know how to change and control vibration. They heal with the laying on of hands. They can communicate with a higher reality, calling down the Holy Spirit in a more proficient manner than the usual Catholic priest, and in practicing what they teach, they adhere as best they can to honesty, chastity, and the discipline of poverty. The way they work is in obvious contrast to the Catholic material sumptuousness and corruption in a two faced system of light and darkness.

The Cathars open hearts and widen minds. However, their original peaceful conduct mutates into the violence of defence under pressure from prelates and a French crusade sent against them. In this dissident sect I recognize only too well the remnants of the Gnostic scriptures in early mystic Christianity, its dualism stemming from the Persian Zoroaster, reported in legend to have lived 6,000 years ago. Add to this their reverence for St. John of the Apocalypse, writing his composite of scriptures in the dank little cave above the sea on the Isle of Patmos. Include the doctrine of Saul of Tarsus, an initiate of the mystery schools before being struck by the lightening of Christian revelation. Mix in some Buddhist tenets as well as a few Thracian Celtic elements, spicing the Cathar doctrine held within the early gothic arch of Christianity, and I picture an aging, wandering pilgrim. He walks in the rags of once-rich Byzantium silk. He collects alms on his way back home to the west from whence he came as a child, helping to carry the treasures of wisdom east from the last sinking lands of Atlantis.

For these devout believers with their concept of dualism in the conflicting forces of Good and Evil, the material world had been created by a demiurge, Lucifer, a fallen spirit. He is equated with the vengeful Jehovah, opposed to the Divine Creator from whom came the Christ. Moreover, as the Christ was an emanation, a shadow sent forth from God, he only appeared human but possessed no physical body that could be crucified as such.

There was no resurrection from crucifixion on a wooden cross, only ascension to His place of origin. The purity of the Virgin Mother was viewed in much the same light. However, the cross, similar to the Egyptian Ankh, a cross surmounted with a sun disk, is used as a symbol of spirit's painful existence in matter. Motivated to seek purity in a manifestation of evil materialism spawned by the Devil, the Cathars, ordained or secular, led spartan lives of integrity with distaste for the tangible. They acknowledged Lucifer, Prince of Darkness, as the foremost angel fallen from Heaven wwho created men of clay without spirit. If God wished to place spirit within this imperfect creation, then God had to let Lucifer do it. And, if Lucifer spawned his own world, he would also rule over God's pure spirits seduced to incarnate in this dominium of matter.

Why God permitted Lucifer this power, the Cathars never really address, and it remains a turbulent question for you, the *Homo sapiens*, since it suggests that God's spirits seduced into this world are essentially pure, in contrast to Lucifer's men of mud!

These robust deviants condemn the Catholic Church and the power of kings and emperors seen as authorities ruled by the Devil, the master of this world that cannot be expected to change. I stand with these people in the elements of nature, as well as in houses and caves. Their wandering teachers, longhaired and pale from fasting, wear belted black robes. They have no churches. I listen as they explain the doctrine of reincarnation and obligatory vegetarianism, due to their flawed understanding that human souls could transmigrate into animal forms, a half-truth at best under certain circumstances.

At the time of death they use their key prayer, the *Consolamentum*, to catapult the soul free from Earth, and re-clothed in light amidst the stars it passes up through the constellations into the bosom of the Father. In a cave lit with white candles I watch intently the inner rites of initiation for both sexes believed to have been created equal in potential and dignity. As usual, theory and practice differ. In this patriarchal society, women, whether healers or initiates, are not allowed to preach, and I find their strength lies in the formidable matriarchs with a social standing higher in Languedoc than in other medieval kingdoms. They are responsible for the religious discipline of their children.

I am with a few of these *Perfecti* when they call down radiant entities into one of the caves. The initiates communicating with these *Bright Ones* view them as a hierarchy of the Eternal who sends out His emanations in divine couples (similar to the ancient teachings in Egypt), an idea transmitted down in the practical habit of the Cathar preachers, the representatives of the Divine, moving about in male pairs conforming to morals and the dangers of travel in that period. In the caves impregnated with the telluric energy of granite, assisting in meditations, trance and contact with other beings, I ask one question: what do they mean when talking about speeding the soul, they call a spark of Light trapped in flesh, back through the stars and constellations to join God? After a considerable silence, a man of many years replies: "We do not stem from this world. Our souls passed throughthe stars and sun created by the Devil, before we were brought here and enchained by the Master of Darkness." I nod, but say nothing.

The crusade has gathered force. Cathars hold fast in their fortress of Montsegur now under siege. Perched on an impregnable rocky peak dropping sheer to the valley, it acts as a funnel of power.
This high and holy magnetic place has been turned from dilapidation into the region's headquarters for their knights, ministers, and congregation guarded by a modest garrison.

They know the meaning of the pentagram, an enriched insignia of Man, his cosmic proportions and relation to the five elements of matter. In the fashion of that era the five-pointed star represented the material, the spiritual, the intellectual, the reasonable, and the substantial. I see its shape in the courtyard by the keep. Its small upper room is empty and ready for the rituals of calling down the Bright Ones. I shall not tell them that some of these projections come from the False Light always there in its polarity to trap and control them.

For thousands of years in this location the guardians of tradition have also honoured the sun and kept this ancient Celtic-Iberian veneration within their Christianity. Old knowledge lives on in the secret core of the Cathar religion. I have also seen Gnostic texts, as well as pre-Christian teachings referring to the sun, the eye of God, the mystic sun behind the sun, source of avatars. The fortress of Montsegur, built to be aligned with the constellation of Bootes with its bright star Arcturus, held the waning wisdom of lost Atlantis alongside Celtic traditions and doctrines from the east.

The French crusaders, mostly men from the north sent to destroy the southern French 'heretics' of Languedoc, besiege us. The Pope and the King of France are furious with the Cathar resistance undermining their authority. Equally, neither faction has forgotten the massacre at one of the most prosperous towns, Béziers, invaded by Catholic crusaders in 1209. They murdered everyone, and celebrated the event in a letter to the Pope saying: "Nearly twenty thousand of the citizens were put to the sword, regardless of age and sex. The workings of divine vengeance have been wondrous." Then as now, I have difficulty in remaining objective in the face of your blind brutalityand observe with deference the courageous people around me. The fortress space is barely adequate for the Perfecti, including knights with family members in the keep, and the garrison. Others, in flimsy huts, clinging to the flanks of the cliffs, endure the cruelties of climate. They prefer their physical discomfort to the Catholic inquisition. Winter is a cold hell. We draw wellwater and light fires     in the forge, bakery, and dwellings. My admiration grows as I watch their faith unite them under stress. Outside our fortress sanctuary, for us a sacred edifice, the Cathar fortitude gains respect from the near 10,000 French crusaders encircling our domain they never cease to batter daily with stone  missiles.

We are under constant threat. Incoming supplies from the faithful have been blocked off in the siege instigated by the pope after a band of wild Cathar knights plotted and succeeded in murdering with mace and hatchet a  delegation  from the Inquisition. At first the killings lighted hope for resistance, only to be transformed into a death knell tolled by the equally-fanatic Catholics. I am exasperated at the way the strength within you Earthlings is always split into opposition. It is as if your receptors for energy function well enough, before your emotion and lower mind divert it into a kill or cure situation, always using violence accompanied by the ridiculous, if not sacrilegious, cry of "God be with  us!"

When will it change? You are largely living on genetic programming with a time lapse to be triggered by you… you who are related to our Galactic strain. Wake up! Think and feel Light; that Light will alter your physical and interdependent psycho-spiritual being. Try to unchain yourselves from guilt, shame, and blame that ignite the furnace of revenge.

The siege continues. Rumours of help have died with the smell of stale smoke in the air. The last hidden path from the fortress has been blocked through treachery. Aided by their women, our last skirmish with the crusaders has failed. The leaders, two knights of powerful families, are both initiates, and one is an alchemist. They decide to negotiate for peace after the ten months of siege.

They obtain a truce for two weeks with surprisingly good terms, providing all renounce their heresy or otherwise be burnt. The truce gives time to prepare for thedeath they have chosen.

None recant and in those last days, others belonging to the garrison voluntarily take vows of allegiance to the Cathar faith. The truce also gives the last chance       to celebrate the spring equinox called Bema. It is officially the death of Mani, the teacher they hold responsible for bringing eastern dualism into early Christianity. It features the doctrine of two opposing principles within creation: God and Light (spirit), thwarted by Darkness and the Devil (the material). Remember that Christianity had won out over the earlier Mithraism, the  soldier's religion  in  which they drank the sacramental blood of the bull. Bema coincides with Easter, originally a pagan festival adopted by you Christians for the time of crucifixion and resurrection echoing the spring celebration of the sun's return after  its  point  of death in the winter solstice. The mythic, solar Christ has his correspondence in the recurring seasonal equinoxes, astronomical phenomena that are transformed into a solar  Christ  myth  accepted  by this sect in their most secret teachings as a symbol  of the eternal Light returning to penetrate the Evil of the manifest world.

In Egypt, thousands of years before the Christianity, the boat of Ra, the Sun god, carries his son, Horus, the awakened cosmic consciousness, across the waters of space. It marks an astrological and astronomical journey in both time and metaphors of spirit. The mythical Horus, the divine teacher in the celestial barque, becomes the historical Jesus, the teller of parables standing in the barque to preach. He says to paraphrase according to your Gospel of Luke:

*There are those who see, hear and understand, and those who do not.*

Before the Easter celebration I meet with the two Lords of Montsegur.

The younger is joined to the elder by marriage to his daughter. The younger, a man, vain of his beauty and inordinately proud to claim ancestry from an ancient Iberian moon goddess, is also a skilled alchemist. It comes to pass that he was later named a traitor and coward when he escaped just before the fortress was entered.

His planned disappearance was for the good of all. He knew too much and could betray many people despite his oath of silence. A risky situation at best for the older lord, spared from burning, when later questioned, died a broken man.

In returning to that night before Bema, when we move to the alchemist's quarters, I feign trance for acceptability as a guardian of ancient knowledge. In short, we review the past and gather anew the heritage from pre-history gleaned for legends and dreams engendered from Atlantis and on through time.

On the night before the truce ends, the fortress is sealed off. Yet three Perfect Ones and a young mountain guide hide with leather saddlebags and ropes in a shallow hollow. Covered with bushes it is hardly perceptible below the wall above the sheerest drop down the valley. Easily disguised, I am the young mountain guide. We descend, carefully, cautiously. Darkness is our second cloak. The following night, during the rampage of crusaders emptying the fortress, the three men each take a bag with money for the Cathar resistance and to pay bribes for the release of prisoners. Each goes his own way. I take the precious Book of the Seven Seals wrapped and sewn in thick cotton under leather. It is less heavy than I thought it would be.

Dawn comes. My time is nearly up. Once below the walls and down the precipice of the rock face, I must make my way through the horror of the whispering crowd, on and up into the forests, rooted against limestone cliffs, to place the book into the hands of a noble woman. I turn away at the memory of those last hours after the truce ends.

On 16 March, 1244, men, women, and children, with the last-minute converts from the garrison, are dragged from the fortress, and in semi-trance they walk to death by fire.

No sound escapes their lips. Herded into a communal wooden stockade, over 200 human souls are pushed into straw lit with tarred faggots. Only the crackle of wood ablaze against the chants of priests and occasional shouts from the crusaders disrupt an awe-inspiring silence. In the holocaust, Cathars from a cultivated aristocracy burn alongside artisans and peasants. I stand and witness through the thick, stinking smoke, flames that lap and roast sizzling flesh.

The pope, complying with holy law, is absolved. The hand of no churchman has spilt blood. Fire was the executioner.

I look with a disgust and sadness greater than the stench in my nostrils, and am touched by the obstinacy of dignified Cathars refusing to break their vows. The victory won by superior numbers is no more than a moral defeat in a nightmare from your reality. The strength of these good people comes from a dream not quite of this world. It will be over seven hundred years, the people predict, before their spirit of dissent will rise again. Turning, I start the cold walk to the forest. It feels almost too long until I see on the open crest of a hill a cloaked figure standing beside a great horse, its steaming nostrils in her hand.

Like myself, beneath her cloak, she is dressed like a man but wears a warrior's mail tunic belted with a short sword. Her hair falls free across her wide shoulders and indeed we know each other. She is an incarnated Keresch, a red headed witch-warrior, already a legendary fighter and lighter of beacons in the hills and hearts of the Cathars, whereas I am no more than a visitor about to depart.

Between us words are not required. She receives the Book of Seals and rides off into the mountains. As the iconic guardian of Montsegur, the inheritance from her father, like your King Arthur, she still sleeps in the hills of the Pyrenees. Her spirit will rise again at the right time.

It has been a contest between two brands of fanaticism, one active, the other basically passive. Both are suffused with power: the Catholics for influence on Earth whereas the Cathars related its use to a higher scheme of things. I have observed and assessed yet, as a Keresch, I must remain calm, allowing only the influence of Origin to move through and around me.

My mission is to deliver the sacred book, not to fight with violence. Unpleasant scenarios of wars and persecution have been repeated again and again. They have attracted ever-recurring bouts of prophecy trumpeting the end of the world and the advent of a saviour coming to redeem the faithful in wicked times.

The events in Montsegur are just another episode showing how vicious forces hold your race in chains. The rule of violence in time will implode in its own metastasis taking as many Earthlings as possible with it.

Should you wish to avoid waiting, to rise or fall, you had better wake up and work not to reincarnate here again unless you choose to have a special mission, first pull yourselves up by your own bootstraps, and then we can help. Rather than depleting yourself by attacking Darkness, work to strengthen the Light.

This dissident but Christian sect, known by several names, also called themselves the Good Men. Their interpretation of Christianity arose in Bulgaria against social conditions and the Byzantian church in the early 10th century. It took hold in France a hundred years later. I tell of their beliefs to unveil forgotten roads travelled in lost times through prehistory into recorded cultures and the creeds of many religions. Their inner doctrines were mixed and mingled with teachings from Atlantis to ancient India, and seeded in nomadic waves of commerce and migrating people.

Threadbare memories became woven into myths. The teachings of Light were more than often corrupted on the way east, past the Caspian Sea, to colonies already settled in mid-Asia before Atlantis vanished. Some went further into what are now places of hissing wind blowing through brittle bones and dunes of sand covering forgotten cities and fertile lands of forgotten ages. In the migrations of peoples from beyond your history, the ancestors of Celtic tribes, a fierce war-like horde, entered western Europe from sinking Atlantis with others moving on eastwards. In their wake they left traces of their genetic strain.

Many centuries later, another wave of red headed men with beards and light eyes appeared in wall paintings along your eastern trade routes. They tell of a mixed Celtic presence relaying goods and persistent beliefs in a hive of cross-pollination. Over time, as the Celts returned in a great circle westward, they passed through Turkey and Macedonia leaving their trace in the Thracian mysteries on their long way back through Europe to rejoin their kind with the Druids in the land once known as Gaul, now France. The Cathars, familiar with the underlying Druidic lore of their terrain, knew that the secrets of the Grail originated from the Celtic cauldron holding the bubbling, living essence of life. The womb filled with blood was represented by the cauldron, an emblem of matter confined and impregnated with life. From the cauldron, the womb of creation came the headwaters of all rivers, or all the ingredients for manifestation.

The Christians, as usual, adopted pagan symbols. They transformed this one into a cup holding your Christ's blood, the mystic vivifying fluid in the body of the Cosmos. It is the solar bloodstream flowing through the lens of your sun to your heart chakra, the seat of the Higher Consciousness exemplified in the teachings of Jesus, named as your last saviour. Perhaps this perspective will give another understanding of your Christian communion of eating the flesh and drinking the blood of your Redeemer that could otherwise be dismissed as spiritual cannibalism. We too have had our Avatars.

They came to change our way of thinking, and the same situation has existed on Earth throughout its history. Their appearance announced the arrival, the influx of a superior energy, to quicken evolution on all levels of life. It stirs those who are ready. The rest have to evolve at their own pace. Were it possible to awaken all humanity at the same time, your history would not be what it is. Often it can be best to just turn people over, and from having nightmares at least they enter sweet dreams. To wake them up is always painful. To retrieve lost memory is seldom without trauma.

In the identity of the Hindu Krishna, an incarnation of the Avatar Vishnu, lies a story concealing genetic characteristics that would have been impossible to explain to Indian scholars at the time of its writing, reputed to have been recorded circa 4th to 5th century BC, after eons of oral tradition. As says Krishna in the Bhagavad Gita:

> I am the Cause. I am the production and dissolution of the whole of Nature. On me
> is all the Universe suspended as pearls upon a string. Even though myself unborn,
> of changeless essence, and the Lord of all existence, yet in presiding over Nature
> which is mine, I am born but through my own mystic power of Self-ideation, the
> Eternal Thought in the Eternal Mind. (ch. VII

Self-born Krishna proclaims what in your world is just beginning to be understood.

All life forms have a genetic blueprint stored in their DNA.

Once the necessary elements are available in the universe, strands of DNA spontaneously come into existence, thus disproving that no structure can occur by itself unless it be by chance.

Recurring spontaneous existence of DNA confirms that life in the universe is not a matter of chance. You could say DNA, if seen through your poetic and magic glasses, is precipitated into your materiality from photons of light that in their streams hold the memory of the genetic and psychic components from all your reincarnations. Vishnu's incarnations as an Avatar include a progression of Buddhas up to the historical figure.

He is foretold to reappear again as Kalki, the Warrior, mounted on a white horse with sword and fire who comes to burn the souls of darkness in your age of the Kali Yuga, the age of greed and false prophets. Krishna, Jesus the prophet, and others before them are examples of incarnations holding this cosmic principle found in every realm wherever there is the presence of Man. I will return later to our two Avatars and the circumstances that led to their appearance.

---

*Accept mixtures of fact, myth, and hidden knowledge. The role of the storyteller is to awaken imagination and bring timelessness into tales that portray the human psyche and the terrible extremes you have enacted throughout your history. Instead, reach out and connect with universal Light in worlds beyond your world.*

*The immutables*

*They came in vortex from the mouth*
*Of cosmic gods with eyes of flame*
*That watched the Salamanders' game*
*Of love with greening, wind-blown Sylphs*
*And Ondines in their siren song.*

*The Merlin Mind then wrought its change,*
*And seeding forms, in Aether's space,*
*Hammered into shape by Gnomes*
*In contrapuntal beat and song*
*So strong, the turning of the Mystic Mills*
*Poured down upon our spinning Earth*
*miracles behind the sun.*

*Keresch children's song.*

*The ancients associated the four elements of creation with Earth as a cube, Water an*
*icosahedron, Fire a tetrahedron, and Air a dodecahedron*

## CHAPTER 7. THE DIVERSITY OF YOUR HERITAGE

On our planet, I am sure you would find many similarities to your own, only more refined, more beautiful, and long-lasting, for we live in a higher frequency with wider perceptions. Our bodies are constituted to receive a much greater inflow of energy than Earthlings, basically because we have not been diminished through genetic meddling. In observing you, we recognize and learn from the unique qualities humans on Earth have forged during eons of intervention, as well as living in a geography no less explosive than your volcanic and insane rages. Few could withstand what you have survived as, I dislike saying, an experimental species.

Far from what you call angels, we are modifying our faults perhaps not fast enough due to an overriding wish to retain our specific characteristics. We show a fierce independence and a dislike of binding ourselves to others, even if we have the same cause. You would term us 'bolshie' at best. We are ready to help when called, providing you leave us alone afterwards. Perhaps our most disconcerting trait is laughter. Our habit is to laugh uproariously when beset by tales of woe and self-pity due to lack of insight leading to misfortune. For example: the people of ..., especially the Chinese, have the infuriating (to you Earthlings) habit of giggling at awkward circumstances; the bigger the catastrophe, the higher their nervous mirth. Admittedly, they copied us eons ago when we infiltrated their culture and noted their inclination to imitate what pleased them. Too often they adopted the form without the content. They laughed to hide their embarrassing inadequacies in dealing with trauma, a reaction hardly similar to our wry sense of humour.

We seldom stayed for long, although occasionally incarnating amongst them. They embody too much of the Anunnaki and retain an ant-like collective mind

However, we were intrigued by the extreme cleverness of their elite combined with an aptitude for the martial arts. We helped them develop a system of training the mind and body in which the subconscious absorbs the directives behind the movements imbued with the telluric power they call the Dragon Force moving through the Earth. The masters of martial arts have connected the subconscious with the supraconscious via daily repetition of movements, until the body becomes automatically fused with the practitioner's will. There are no shortcuts. Should you wonder about the Japanese Samurai, need I tell you that after we had taught them, their best could match us providing our height was compatible with their size. While on the subject of the Asians, many of their folk tales recount stories of humans taken down into palaces below the water or sea where dragons, the dilong connected to Earth and Water, granted them favours and mated with women to produce half-human dragon children. From the earliest recorded times, the haughty emperors spoke of themselves as literally Sons of the Dragon and Sons of Heaven. With the Chinese dragon belonging to both Earth and Heaven and all four elements, it brings forth an association with genetic engineering from two sources in an image incorporating the positive and negative in a twisting ladder linking the Light and the Dark in an extraterrestrial heritage.

Myths can be read on many levels, more than ever today, with extraterrestrial genetic manipulations in mind. You may ask if Alien Dragon Reptilians successfully procreate with humans? Either way, the famous/infamous serpent/dragon power indicates Aliens, including Anunnaki of all persuasions, fiddling with the planet's auric grid, its electromagnetism as well as human chromosomes.

We, the Keresch, know only too well the humanoid Cysts. They want the *Bridge* to immortality, the birthright of Galactic man, but omitted by the Anunnaki in their genetic manipulations begetting a near-mindless slave race, and other gruesome creatures in their experiments. More successfully, the Anunnaki often turned cloned humans into zombies. Or, in a different category, like the Reptilians, they could overshadow your mind in demonic possession, and attempt to maim the connection with your *Immortal Flame*. However, possession by any entity must not be confused with psychological disturbances based on abnormal abnormal changes in a person's character.

At present, many accounts of the Reptilians crowd your areas of curiosity. It is for you to decide if you wish to be drawn to this subject. Let me instead speak about more attractive entities of your environment. The Ancients used the Mystec Elements, the immutable substances of Earth, Air, Fire, and Water as similes for the qualities of various states of energy- composing matter. In the magic of your imagination, picture Fire forging matter, Water giving it birth, Air donating it life, and Earth imparting form in the fifth Element of space, or Ether, that provides the place for growth and change.

Your body holds Water in its secretions; Fire in the heat of flesh and blood, and Earth in the body's inorganic constituents; Air is present in its chemical components; and the forces of Ether run through the subtle energy system of the meridians. The Elements, known in your world, are like shadows cast off from their origin. The fifth element of Ether will soon be better understood, with two more to be discovered in the far distant future of Earth's transmutation.

Imagine these Elements as streams of energy, each one an abode for many embodied entities who have their limited existence there: Nature Spirits, temporary manifestations without human self-consciousness and with only one of the elements in their constitution. They belong to a multitude of categories with a multitude of functions within their specific element.

A change of function also brings a change of name, so frequently noted in the references given to the Nature Spirits in your pre-Christian cultures. Philosophically, they could also be regarded as universal principles reflected in nature and in man. In tribal communities all over your planet, shamans continue a dialogue with the invisible spirits in the oldest recognition of the unseen powers behind material tangibility. They praise and propitiate them in rituals and ceremonies. These spirit entities precipitated from the matrix of Nature can be intelligences of considerable power, capable of using the polarity of destruction and preservation often at their capricious will. Drawn into your rituals, the greater the emotional content, the better it is for them. They feed on the full range of human feelings, from violent hatred to ecstasy. Remember the story

69

of Peter Pan and his fairy friend Tinker Bell; on finding her light fading she asked all the children in the world to clap hands and save her from dying. She needed the energy of their recognition and love.

Few Earthlings can see fairies, fewer now than in times past. It used to be normal and just considered another way of seeing between the veils of frequencies, thicker now, no doubt, due to your general disbelief in spirits of anything. Fairies envy you humans for your core of immortality that they lack. When I have spoken with the pleasant ones, like children, they feel deprived of your sympathy and recognition for their work in helping the evolution of your Earth. On opening your senses you will perceive them. The Beautiful Ones, the ancient Nature Spirits, can give you help in healing. You need them, and they need you. You share the planet, so sit with them and listen.

Fairies are associated with the Elements: gnomes of the Earth, sylphs of the Air, Water for undines, Fire for the salamanders. Together with the violent elementals, perpetual shape-shifters personifying Nature's disruptive powers, they are like all of their kind, without man's self-determinism or *Immortal Flame*.

Their instinct, as yet not developed into a human intelligence, leaves them similar to psychic embryos with only latent reasoning to curb their mischief when they so want. Many are your folk tales of changelings, the human babies kidnapped by fairies in search of what makes you different from them. Similar stories are reminiscent of current, but in comparison, unpleasant abduction by Aliens with the same goal. In some respects, the gods of old were embodiments of Nature's forces, seen by psychics and worshipped in fear. At other times, the so-called gods belonged to the family of Man.

They were high initiates, incarnated or visiting extraterrestrials, capable of bending the elementals to their will. Often they were Merlin, the archetype Magician, striding through myth and legend. He was an interdimensional time traveller with many reflections. His immense intelligence beyond your comprehension created his own game, here and elsewhere. His power manipulated minds using both Darkness and Light according to his agenda.

He was the Great Beguiler, the Deceiver who implants dreams, supported by machines of artificial intelligence, and whose dominance can only be escaped by activating your knowingness and self awareness relayed through your opened heart chakra. Picture Moses, in another myth, his beard and hair blown by the gales, as he commands the waters of the Red Sea to part.

Exaggerated, at best, it is another half-truth. There is little evidence in Egypt of the Israelites remaining as slaves in that terrestrial land. Originally brought in as a workforce they were integrated into Egyptian life, and often with the name of *Moses* (the name itself derived from the Egyptian root without the prefix for example, Tut mos, or Ra mos) held high positions with great wealth and power. Excavations in Palestine give no record of Israel being born from an Egyptian exodus, but points to it having been taken over by settlers from the Canaanite population in the second millennium BC.

The story is used as an image for leaving the prison of Earth for the higher dimension of the Promised Land, reached through the parting of the waters of space. It covers a hidden truth in an analogy that ignites awe for the magician/leader and his ability to guide a chosen people, the awakened, to a glorious land of milk and honey. The chosen people were the Egyptians themselves. The teaching was one of ascension historically and ethnically misappropriated.

You of Earth need your myths. You should continue to create them when trapped in materialistic societies that do their best to destroy imagination. The relevance of myth is being removed from your lives. With it goes its gift of being drawn into an extended world of archetypes, inspiring you with an identity larger than your passing personality. Visiting extraterrestrials (not always interdimensional, meaning they came from the same density but a different place) comprise another category in a plethora of various types. They include humanoid species, each with their agenda, helpful or harmful depending on their evolution. What about insects? Seek and you will discover that certain Koisan peoples of Southern Africa bowed down before the great praying mantis as their god.

The three streams of beings touching your planet were: first, extraterrestrial and interdimensional man; secondly, mankind developed on Earth from various Galactic strains, and, thirdly, entities of nature belonging to, as your fairy tales tell, the frequencies of Earth, Air, Fire, and Water. Other so-called gods were evolved extraterrestrials as well as interdimensional beings incarnating or visiting your planet. Some came millions of years ago to help the prototype Earthlings in their transformation from shadowy, ethereal, astral beings, still devoid of self-consciousness, when the Earth was a Garden of Eden, and the vegetable kingdom held sway. They were drawn into Earth's condensing atmosphere for further evolution leading to the birth of the animal kingdom and the future receptacle of human consciousness. Others, from different star systems alien to the path of Light, at one point, came for reasons of experiment and power, hoping to make a human species subservient to their wants and needs. It caused inter- galactic wars. It caused split allegiances between many Galactic races, not always human in shape.

All interdimensional beings are, when needed, capable of modifying their density and working on Earth for limited periods before withdrawing to their own realms. Then, as Earth solidified and interpenetration between dimensions hardened, some of our Galactic brothers tell of one mighty Son of the Dreamers. He was so powerful that he did his best in the later times of Atlantis to close forever the gates of the higher realms from Earth and its progeny. He wished to turn your world into a prison. The Earth's surrounding protective grid was altered. He has, to a large extent, been successful.

When it was important for their experiments, these intruders, as well as the Anunnaki and all experts in genetics, could incarnate in the human bodies they had produced through cross-breeding with the Daughters of Earth. A programme of this kind need not necessarily be a negative activity. Earthlings crossed with Galactic of good intent definitely improved the experiment. However, if dominated by unscrupulous Aliens, the cross became a vehicle for their bloodline, their power base. Another occupation with techniques as prevalent today as ever before, involves the control of a human mind in turning the person into a robot. Furthermore, there is the invasive process of a person being possessed for a time by another intelligence, an occurrence common in many tribal societies, dismissed by your physicians under the heading of multiple personalities, in itself a valid condition, but different from being taken over by an external entity. Likewise, educated, sophisticated people also fall into this latter category when a secret portal in their psyches opens, allowing their normal sense of identity to be overridden in mind and body by an invasive being, sometimes a Nature Spirit, or an ancestor from another density that temporarily invades the physical form.

Other experiments produced bodies animated with the Spark of Life plus a basic cellular intelligence that, with these two essential constituents of a material vehicle, were clones ready to receive a reduced human presence, or be left as encoded robots. Too many of the dark Anunnaki, with their experience of manipulating the physics of this world, revered nothing and no one above themselves.

Many of the Aliens had brilliant and powerful minds, but above all love did not enter their agenda. Somehow even with knowledge of enlightenment, they preferred to rule, as it were, from Darkness rather than Light. Other human-like extraterrestrials had neither the ability to touch the face of Origin, nor experience a wide range of emotions since they did not have within them the Bridge to an Immortal Flame. They only had the intelligence of a brilliant, material mind, and at worst, in their lack they continue to bring horror to Earth that in your 14th century prompted the Italian poet, Dante, to compose his epic work, The Inferno, in which he writes:

*Over the gates of hell stand God's words: I too in my Wisdom created this.*

Even on your planet, as did the Cathars, some so-called heretics claim that if Light can create, so by God's permission can Darkness, and all soul-seeds return to their source when the Universe sleeps at the end of the giant cycles of manifestation. In Light there is Darkness, and in Darkness, Light, both belonging to a mysterious unity. A mysterious unity indeed. However, you Earthlings should not sink into a comfortable attitude in which evil practices are tolerated in the short term because in the wider picture they have a place and need not be opposed or condemned. The devil, you might decide, does not exist… it is all in the imagination… don't get involved… do nothing.

Those in misery are justly reaping the results of their acts; this world and its people can never be changed. Instead, become aware of the paradox at the heart of this concept, for true as it is in one way, change exists in the ability to change yourself and your point of view in the face of any circumstance. Alter your vibration and it will bring a different reality.

Evolved Beings of Light were horrified at the travesty of Man being brought into existence in the laboratory of Earth, first using a species of early, ape-like humans in the experiment. At one point, the Legions of Light decided to transfer a part of themselves to these human parodies, a transmission that we, the Keresch, call the *Bridge*, the one attribute that distinguishes humans from animals. Even so there is a latent self-consciousness, the recognition of the self in apes and certain birds. Man knows, and he knows that he knows.

"There but for the grace of God go I!" you could well exclaim on meeting the inquisitive eye of an orangutan in the forests of Kalimantan. With his budding self-consciousness and commendable intelligence, he is at present unable to do calculus or contact his nascent *Higher Mind*. He has instinct rather then inspiration. How near and yet so far is the ape from us with apparently such a mysteriously tiny, one per cent difference in our genetic composition. How might a great Galactic view us? Are we clever little pets capable of performing circus tricks with the mind while our evolved brethren understand astrophysics at birth? The thought is hilarious if not downright dumbfounding. The answers are legion, and yours will reveal the quality over the quantity of your intelligence. Although the invisible fountain of creation appears to be very far away when on your planet, it is but an illusion, a manner of thought better abandoned if you Earthlings are to awaken. Think of the distance being no wider, no longer, and no deeper than the distance travelled in thought. Turn your attention inwards and all distance vanishes. You can be in a circle or point of light the instant you think it. This is where meditation in the path of saints and mystics ought to lead you, although, understandably, the state of your planet at present, so sensitive to the increasing chaos of your emotions, aggravates your sense of disorder and loss.

Remember Earth's biomass membrane is affected by the quality of your thoughts and feelings. We, the Keresch, know well the effort needed to keep faith with the inner flame.

---

*Absorb what you can and leave the rest for another time. You are growing at*
*your own rate and will always reconnect with what you already know*
*in your heart about the Elements, Fairies, Extraterrestrials and Interdimensional beings.*

*Extract from 'A Record'*

*None sees the slow sure upward sweep*
*By which the soul from life depths deep*
*Ascends - unless mayhap, when free*
*With each new death we backward see*
*The long perspective of our race,*
*Our multitudinous past lives trace*
*since first as breath of God*
*through space*

*William Sharp 1855- 1905*

## CHAPTER 8. THE CORE OF THE MATTER

Each sunrise back in my home I give praise to our Dreamers. From them came the First-Born Sons of the Central Spiritual Sun. Their mind, collective or individualised, conceived ideas given substance through a hierarchy of beings, embodied according to the frequency of where they were. They were the architects within their particular portion of the universe. You can call them a category of Cosmic Man who exists in higher densities, a good word as it infers a vibration, and frequency rather than a place.

It is difficult to describe this process of creation in linear terms because time and space are not what you normally think they are. It is as if one space can have many times and time can have many spaces all at once. You speak of wavelengths in a hierarchy of place: high, low, short, long, instead of conceiving them before differentiation, as a whole spectrum superimposed in and coexistent with one another. You Earthlings often equate various wavelengths, vibrations, and densities with parallel universes in which your other self, or selves, can exonerate themselves in different timelines, while you muddle along in the everyday events of this world. It is a way of accepting different states of being and of consciousness in your linear sense of time. We are all shards, splinters of ourselves, that ultimately we must bring together.

Imagine you come with me to my planet, into our landscape and family home. We walk up to the revolving Tower of Contemplation and at dawn you join me in giving praise to Shiva dancing with the Sun of Life in all the worlds. As the vast Expander, the Transformer, he dances with one foot raised while the other stands still at the node of no motion, in the rise and fall of vibrating waves in hyperspace. Imagine that the loom of his hair holds the warp and woof for the vertical and horizontal interaction of electric interaction of electric and magnetic energies with their countless patterns showing every manifestation within the mind of Cosmic Man.

Look out onto our fertile land veined with streams. Our crops are good. We leave large cities for other cultures for we prefer to work with our hands, study hard, play music, dance, and live simply, surrounded by beauty. Beyond the rich lands you will see the desert, its rocks, the tinted sands and volcanic outcrops engemmed with stones. The sands are carpeted with spring flowers where flocks of butterflies shimmer in swarms so large they can block the light. Yes, look! There run the herds of thunder-hoofed wild horses, some with wings, white as milk, copper red and shiny, black as jet. We ride them, or rather they carry us, at our mutual pleasure. The wild heart of the horse is free, and that freedom is expressed in its unpredictability. We live with our animals in a state of symbiosis. From minerals to organisms, to all sentient life and man, our energy is combined into a living net, a grid of consciousness around the planet. Observe it here and remember it is the same on Earth. Only you, seldom by ignorance but by greed, disrupt the process.

I now take your arm and we descend to my private room north of our meeting hall. As you observe, we live in a large white compound built from an amalgamation of mineral and vegetable substance honed and polished to perfection in a molecular astuteness to keep our home at a perfect temperature. Ours is a large two-storied oblong with an inner balcony and large court with a shallow decorative pool, its waters rippled by a fountain. Four flowering trees stand at each corner. We like simplicity in private life that you might call spartan, and take delight in manual work we find relaxing after pursuing science combined with psychic power as taught in our halls of learning.

That we have different Elements changes the form of our matter, and in one way you could think of matter as form and substance. Form changes shape. Substance remains the same, although the ratio of ingredients differs with others added in the dominion of the higher frequencies.

We incarnated with many other Galactics, and our spaceships were shown in paintings of that extraordinary period of the Renaissance. Then, in Constantinople where philosophy from ancient Greece held hands with Arab medicine and mathematics only partially from ancient Greece held hands with Arab medicine and mathematics only partially known in Europe, when this extended knowledge and commerce entered Italy in 1434 with the Chinese fleet sailing into Venice, it brought a veritable bazaar of East meeting West. On arrival in Florence it influenced a bevy of extraordinary men in the way they thought and questioned, traded and used politics. It introduced new ideas into your world's habitual viciousness interspersed with the arts, the dagger, and the dance. Whole groups incarnated to urge forward your progress by circulating information through the invention of the printing press, comparable to the revolution of the Internet today. Speaking of Earth, lower your eyes to our patterned floors of wood or stone. They hold inlaid mandala illustrating how thought forms are wrought into objective reality. Others show the dimensional portals, and in contemplation they activate our·higher faculties, and accompanied by the vocabulary of music, we tune in.

With us, unlike on Planet Earth, science and the arts are enmeshed and in painting or sculpture we make no distinction between artist and artisan.
At present, people in your worldpromoting ugliness and violence and suppressing beauty and other old fashioned virtues, theemptiness in your spiritual diet will be filled with the junk food of psychic control from Hollywood, the press and other master manipulators of public culture. Come follow me into my private room, intimate and domed for sound.

Sit at ease. Choose your comfort. Listen to the simplicity of flutes in the wind, or if you wish, any of your own music, and smile, for this is a place of healing. We use imagination, breath control, and the frequencies of our six Elements, each carrying its innate colour, sound, and geometry. The kind and degree of energy needed in relation to the patient, we pull directly out of the atmosphere. It is not necessarily channelled through our bodies, as do your healers who often suffer fatigue. I will tell you as much as is possible of knowledge central to our understanding of who and what you are. The history on Earth for the last 12,000 years has been one of forgetfulness, reinforced with false and manipulated facts, imposed hundreds of years before your Christ. But rest now in the dream of this finer reality. Remember you will remember. It is already known in the five-pointed embryonic etheric pentagram in your heart.

With the current rush into your New Age philosophies, much is explained in a new vocabulary, but too often the baby is thrown out with the bathwater. Accumulated wisdom is rejected together with legitimately outworn theories. You forget to ask an essential question: "What have I learnt from any experience, good or bad?" No answer comes without recall, and without an answer there are no signposts on your road. Memory is a reminder, an indicator to what you have assimilated in the art of living and once the essence from memory has been educed, you need no longer gargle in your own bathwater, but can live in the eternal present, the point, the place, and the space that passes from tunnels of inversion into passages of expansion.

*Think of the present as the ever-passing moment that can never be repeated.*

We take pleasure in our tonal vocabulary, particularly in the reading of poetry. Please close your eyes and listen while I speak Keresch. You will grasp perfectly, because although you think you have forgotten, you have not. Similar to shards from a broken urn, the long-gone words will reassemble themselves into shape.

I will begin with what is familiar to you: Greek mythology. It is so human in more senses than one, with gods as violent, capricious and selfish as you Earthlings! They speak of the twins, Castor and Pollux, in a simple tale with hidden meaning, usually comprehended only in its outer form. The brothers are twins, differing in one vital aspect. One has been given a divine gift from the benevolent gods, opposed to the other castrating deities competing with each other on your planet. The twin Castor represents the human constitution with only the material intelligence as his guide. His brother Pollux is granted the added psychic principle of the *Higher Mind*. Bound and limited to his material mind and deprived of his brother's higher principle, Castor dies and goes to the underworld, leaving Pollux, a demigod, to commune with their maker Zeus. Pollux is, however, allowed to visit his brother in Hades, a synonym for Earth. Another enduring tale of magic and adventure is the story of the magician Prospero. He commands Ariel, a captive, bright spirit and his opposite, the deformed, dark-plotting demon Caliban, perpetually railing against his master. Twin spirits they are, Castor and Pollux, or Caliban and Ariel. Our stories keep The Twins separated, whereas with Man, The Twins live together in the same physical being. They are two separate principles in your psychic constitution that I will do my best to explain.

---

*Think of Castor and Pollux as two aspects of your being which are together with your body but different and separate from the flesh.*

*Within the Khat, your physical frame, stand
the components of a temple holding
the structure of your immortality.*

*Keresch teachings*

## CHAPTER 9. PSYCHIC CONSTITUTION

As young Keresch, when we are instructed in the seven facets of Man, our priests use their own archaic words. I will translate them in ancient Egyptian slightly altered from what was pronounced in Atlantis.

1.  We begin with the *KHAT*, the physical body enlivened by its *Spark of Life* from the primordial Cosmic Fire, placed in the physical form which also harbours a subtle, unseen body called the *KHAIBIT*.

2.  The *KHAIBIT* is threaded with unseen circuits in a network of subtle energy that affects the physical body. This intangible sheath holds the invisible kundalini, the chakras and the meridians of acupuncture that form its structure. The *KHAIBIT* is often termed the astral body, the double, the doppelgänger, or the shade of the physical vehicle. The Egyptians, in preserving the corpse, knew that in keeping the *KHAIBIT* connected to the physical body it acted as a spirit guardian in the tombs. Keeping the *KHAIBIT* attached was also an act of protection. If left as a drifting, decaying shell, it could be entered by demons living in what you term the lower astral realms, and used for their unpleasant pleasure of duping people during spirit séances. Your pyramid texts say, with reference to these tricksters in the lower regions that include the Earth and its array of spirit entities:

    *O Devourer of shadows who comes forth from the cave.*

3. The *KA*, the principle of the *Lower Mind*, has the cellular cleverness governing the physical body. Its seat, or portal, is the liver. In its higher function it acts as the intelligence, directing levels of consciousness (the subconscious and unconscious) with the insistence and aptitude of the worldly ego that nonetheless lacks direct contact with the higher densities. The *KA*, housed in its subtle body, the *KHAIBIT*, remains attached to the physical body for as long as it is alive. The *KA* is both positive and negative: the positive part leaves the body in sleep and projects itself into other realms, leaving the remaining negative part to maintain the body's functions. Similar to a Nature Spirit, the *KA* when released from its sheath, if taken up into the new astral body of the deceased, is transformed in an event we call the first ascension of an Earthling having tamed his *Lower Mind* to rise with him into a higher state.

*O KA of shining resurrection! say the pyramid texts.*

In time the *KA* evolves into a separate, self-conscious entity that has been schooled by its master. If adepts of the negative forces capture the *KA* of a living person, often with the help of paralysing poisons, the victim becomes a mindless zombie. Normally at death, when the ectoplasmic cord holding it to the physical body breaks, the *KA* returns to the lower density from where it came before entering into a human reincarnation, whereas the *KA* of an evolved individual, drawn up into his or her new astral form, continues its work and evolution as a sentient being. The next principle is:

4. The BA, your Higher Mind, the Watcher watching you, is the super-physical essence of the astral constitution. Its seat in the flesh is the heart. The BA, represented by the winged hawk, is the emblem of Horus, the Egyptian god of cosmic consciousness and ascension. It comes from

beyond duality but when incarnating registers duality, not to be confused with polarity, essential for manifestation.

Horus, the *BA* principle, emanates from *Origin* and must not be confused with the *KA*. Only when you see yourself in dreams are you in the body of your *BA* and become the Watcher watching your own shadow self. The BA is the connection to your Immortal *Flame* that never incarnates but projects or reflects its Light via the *BA-Bridge* into the incarnated being.

5.   The *SAHU*, or sheath of the *BA*, like any body, has its spark of life and the appropriate principle of the *KA*, needed in any embodiment until beyond manifestation in the realms of spiritualised matter. After this, no vehicle is needed unless desired for exceptional reasons in a lower density.

In certain cases the *BA* in its sheath (or body) can be the visible form of a god assumed. The *BA*, the *Higher Mind*, is the incarnating negative aspect of the positive *Immortal Flame* that never leaves its source. The *BA*, also portrayed as the Phoenix, represents resurrection and the power of transformation.

6.   When in full contact with its *Flame*, the *BA* becomes an *UPS-UN* in the higher densities, at which point it has no need of a body unless to accomplish a special mission. In its evolution the *UPS-UN* is finally drawn up with its life spark and is transformed into *Flame*, named:

7.   The *SEKHEM*: the un-manifest, immortal Spirit.

The higher principles of the *BA* in its sheath, the *SAHU*, contain the germ of Cosmic Man. In certain cases the four, lower principles; the *KHAT*, the material body with its *Spark of Life* coming from the primordial Cosmic Fire and its shadow body, the *KHAIBIT* housing the *KA*, breed the Elementals and the Nature Spirits that are sometimes named the Shadows of the Gods; an inference to them having been precipitated from the cast- off *KAs* of a certain hierarchy of interdimensional Man, the Architects. In this case, their elemental creations have the *Spark of Life* but not the *Flame of Eternity*.

The ultimate ascension takes place when Man reaches the stage of being in total phase with his *Flame*. At this homecoming to *Origin*, Man is beyond reincarnation. The *Flames* are of a brilliance and intensity enough to blind and burn anyone on Earth. From this state of Light, they appoint other beings as their representatives to incarnate, by choice, as great teachers working in the realms of denser manifestations.

Some say our soul-seed has to know the muddy depths of matter before the return journey back to *Origin* in the eternal bosom of the *Immortal Flame*. We *Keresch* teach that having been created as individual Flames, we reach our fullness not by being absorbed, but by absorbing *Origin* into us, and can also become part of a group mind.

> *Many are the gods fallen into physical matter but how many men of Earth have become gods?*

You, who have awoken, give thanks to your ancestry, the *DNA* of your soul, and the memory of your stellar imprints. You are the result of this heritage and have the right to its shield of Light. The *DNA* of your soul's constitution is the template of your being and racial lineage. Think of it as the spirit's marking being vertical and the human as horizontal.

You are indeed a cross.

Human cloning, for example, would symbolically give the horizontal *KA*, without the vertical *BA*, the bridge to *Spirit*. If falling into despair at the amnesia in your world causes the constant repetition of violence and mad behaviour, remember that individuals in touch with their *BA*, by their presence alone, make an impact on their surroundings. When we and other star-seed races incarnate on your planet, it leaves an imprint on the cellular intelligence. The star seed's intrinsically awakened presence and connection with the *BA* in an Earth body, provokes hereditary change in the genome quicker than was possible in the original Anunnaki slave species. Today more than before, despite your mixed heritage and bruised constitution, any advantageous change made in your genome liberates your race.

An enlightened *KA*, even if not taken with you at death, can incarnate in a better state to care for the physical body to which it will be attracted. Think about this and you will glimpse the importance of why we, the Keresch, incarnate here with the long- term view beyond our passing discomfort.

What we learn in your world is retained in our *Higher Mind* and shared with others of our galactic soul seed with its coded DNA. It all adds to any kind of future connections we might choose to have on Earth. You have come with me into my dream and now must return to yours. I have given you the myth of The Twins and its related information, knowing well how in your native setting for the first 40 days after birth the newborn infant recalls in a dream state the lessons learnt during its previous reincarnation.

Dreams they are, because those who wished to enslave humanity imposed conditions in your world that erases the past in the process of birth... exceptions proving the rule. How many of you believe in reincarnation? How many believe in its possibility without scientific proof? The late Dr Ian Stevenson of Perceptual Studies at the University of Virginia has given proof more readily accepted today than when his extended findings were published in 1996, with later meticulous research giving evidence that children with exceptional recall had unusual abilities, illnesses, phobias and philias which could not be explained by the environment or heredity. You walk the razor's edge between the scientists' proposed reality and the unfashionable but perennial lure of ancient beliefs that are becomming systematically more viable.

Time has come to withdraw and contemplate, not just thinking about this information, but also feeling it. To recapitulate the seven principles of man: 1. The KHAT, the physical body with the Spark of Life. 2. The KHAIBIT, the subtle shadow body housing the KA. 3. The KA, or Lower Mind. 4. The BA, or Higher Mind. 5. The SAHU, subtle body of the Higher Mind. 6. The UPS-UN, when the BA is in full contact with Flame.

7. The SEKHEM, the un-manifest Flame of Spirit residing in Origin. It may simplify things if you regard yourself in the classic terminology of body, KHAT, soul, KA, and spirit BA, the bridge to your immortal essence in Origin

## CHAPTER 10. OUR WORLD OF THE KERESCH

At present, when some of your physicists find themselves on the edge of mysticism, it causes problems as much with them as with metaphysicians. The latter claim that mysticism, having lasted for so long in its insights, should stand on its own feet unexplained by science, slipping along on the shifting sands of various contemporary theories. On the other hand, your Sanskrit texts, originating from extraterrestrial contacts and incarnated adepts, have been voiced anew by your cosmologists. In the prayers of praise from the Rig Veda, the cosmological measurements are found to be remarkably close to those of contemporary research.

In your world at this time (one could say that at each level of the created world) nature appears to apply certain mathematical ratios. Until now the golden mean has been understood to be the primary ratio employed by nature in this process. Recently other ratios have been proposed as being the primary ratio; most notably the square root of 2, because such a ratio applied to create spirals or vortices actually has a zero point where other ratios do not. Then again, nature, in its infinite complexity of expression, cannot always be codified this way. Certain ratios create certain spirals and vortices, which appear to hold life together, so whether there is a single mathematical ratio underlying all life remains to be seen.

For your entertainment, I will give you an abbreviated account of our education in which many methods could be applicable in your world.

Within months of our birth we learn about the constitution of our being. Schooling begins with the story of creation, later expanded into physics beyond your ken, especially as one of our elements has not come into existence on Earth. When young, we absorb the principles presented as marvellous tales to awaken imagination and to kindle memory from past existence. Should we lose this sense of amazement, a part of our awareness atrophies and we become diminished on every level.

We teach by encouraging our young to ask questions, not drilling them to chew on facts. We ask them to imagine a point, a dot that could expand to encompass macrocosms. And passing into and through that dot opens vistas of microcosms, each like a mirrored fractal of the All. They picture molecules and atoms that dance, mingle, separate, and alter their combinations. In their orbits and spin, similar to the activity of solar systems, they see in macrocosm to microcosm the meaning of 'as above so below.' The biggest can be similar, though not the same as the smallest, allowing the order of magnitude to produce variation. I gasped when first asked to picture a whirlwind, rushing out from a double vortex of simultaneous expansion and contraction that gives birth to a myriad of stars, in a process beginning beyond my capacity to fully assimilate. I apprehended it in my young heart before this activity became heat, light, and sound falling from the most ethereal of substances into the densest consolidation of matter in motion. We are primarily taught to see things in our mind before reading about them. At present, it is difficult for you Earthlings to fully understand, being limited by your inner and outer environment. Instead, let your children imagine Space as a great ocean, seas upon seas churned into curds by waves of Light that bring forth mists coagulating into suns and planets. The reliefs on the walls of the main temple in Ankor Wat, Cambodia, in beautiful metaphor, depict this eternal scene of churning the milky seas into curds of manifestation, enfolding the interconnection of all life.

No one is an island unto himself. All things are permutations of vibrational energy. But the word 'all' causes difficulty because, like binary opposites, it includes the lower and the higher, the black and the white. Each are opposed in the short term, yet, in the end, the one cannot exclude the other.

For us everything has a place, and providing opposites keep to their space and do not threaten others, we accept their presence in the chessboard of existence. Just as our innate telepathic ability can, if chosen, connect us in happiness or sorrow with friends, it also means we can be aware of unpleasant things. All aspects are connected in space and time, and time in space.

We can speak as mystics or scientists. We choose the former for ease because it can conjure up personal images and individual perceptions of vastness extending outwards and inwards as if entering a hologram, later understood through mathematics and the meaning of ciphers.

First inspired by metaphoric image and our innate aptitude for music and rhythm, we soon join the arts to the beauty of science and the elegance of abstractions. In learning anything, be it history or everyday information, we give the greatest importance to the application of knowledge, especially when it comes to interaction between others and ourselves. All the righteous thoughts and sentiments are valueless if not put into practice, ostensibly in times of stress. Not being perfect we often fail!

While still young, returning one afternoon from my schooling and hearing voices from our tribal court arena built in the heart of our settlement, I wanted to enter. Not wearing the white robes obligatory for public hearings, I remained in the archway. At least three couples were there to present their grievances including Oschka, a mature man, and one of our most valiant fighters.

Impeccable in his unwavering faithfulness to a purpose or to a person, he had had as his devoted youth, Mynu, still learning the arts of war and life. Oschka the mighty had been maimed in battle and Mynu, his companion in allegiance, had perished.

Saddened by the misfortune of Oschka, I meandered off to console myself by walking deep into the forest. In its shadows grew the singing company of great trees radiating their intermingling auras, and their leaves, spattered in sunlight, cupped seasonal flowers or fruit bright and ripe with life that filled my heart with happiness.

Our presence with any type of vegetation releases an exchange of data. Whatever our emotions are, plants absorb our emanations. If you knew the communication between plants, their particular kind of intelligence, as for instance in the case of mushrooms, you would find it almost frightening. Their visible shape is only their reproductive organs growing beneath the soil, and sending out a network of extensions that act similar to the dendrites in your brain, they relay ecological information exchanged with other plant forms in a cellular intelligence you underestimate due to your limited perception of communication between non-verbal life forms. Mushrooms interconnect through an underground vegetal network leaving some plants above ground attuned to the electromagnetic impulses from the stars.

Earthlings may be astonished to know that you are closer to the DNA of mushrooms than to the life-bringing bacteria transported here in the crashed debris of meteorites and comets entering your solar system. That afternoon I sat under a venerable old tree similar to your chenar, and leaned back against the trunk releasing energy to regulate the heart and blood pressure. I closed my eyes until, feeling observed, I awoke to find an antelope in inquisitive enough to lick my feet. They have no fear of man, and as children we are encouraged to make friends with all creatures by developing sympathy and telepathy. In my home, my golden cat rising to my shoulder walks on her hind feet beside me, emitting throaty noises I fully understand. There is more trouble with people disagreeing about their pets than quarrelling among themselves. On my return home for the family•s evening meal we discussed Oschka's situation, his health and loss in battle during the unexpected attack of the Cysts, only a short time ago.

Naturally I listened to my elders' recollections with interest. In a sudden furious attack they had invaded our valley and had teemed down the dark mountains in their reptilian legions mounted on bat-winged robotic triangles bombarding us with undulating spears of electric power that hissed like a myriad serpents. They were astonished to find our people ready in an instant; in battle formation our warriors' tactics avoided much of the direct thrust of the enemy. We flowed in ever- changing formations, parting, reforming, moving forward, or retreating in unpredictable patterns that thwarted the enemy. Our swords and Mavelins, lethal in their magnetic power, our shields radiating deadly impulses, and our commanders, giving verbal or telepathic orders, elegantly outmanoeuvred the invaders. The finale came when our ranks of women surrounding the field moved to high ground between the Cysts and our men.

Turning long trumpets towards the Reptillians they blew the death blast, and, stunned if not killed, the invaders lay enfeebled in their own dark liquids, foul odour and screams of defeated rage. Oschka the mighty loped between the dead and dying, followed by his men and Amazons searching out survivours for interrogation or to terminate their life. In the clash of battle he heard a shrill cry behind him.

He turned. Mynu, not in his obligatory place either beside or behind him, had sped without permission to aid a young Amazon dragged down by four slithering Cysts appearing from under a pile of their slain. Had Mynu informed Oschka of his intent instead of rushing from his place without notice, the two men would have fought the four Reptillians together.

Instead, the young Amazon, having killed two of her adversaries, had fallen stunned by a blow from her other humanoid adversary. Mynu, agile as he was, rushed to her aid. He spun and twisted. He cut into the eyes of the nearest Cyst with his long sword then slipped in slime. Unbalanced, he was swiftly decapitated. His head fell, face down into the filth of the fray before Oschka could arrive. With an age of experience and the restraint of never letting his emotions blind him, Oschka drew the remaining Reptillian towards him.

In moments like this he stayed calm and as emotionally unattached as possible. Throughout his martial training he had been taught never to fight filled with anger or revenge. If he had to kill, killing should be done in a neutral frame of mind impartial to the act itself. Negative emotions, the greater their intensity, give psychic energy to the enemy as well as rebounding on the warrior should he forget his training to keep an outward relentlessness balanced by an inner imperturbability.

Oschka retreated with feigned fear, offering his prized shield and sword as booty, if left to flee. The Reptillian curled before leaping. Oschka knelt under his shield, and in well-simulated whimpers he waited. At the last moment, as the Cyst raised his double-headed searing hot axe, our great warrior slashed his blade tempered with a radiating force up through the protective covering of his antagonist's belly.

The screeching humanoid reptile fell forwards over Oschka, knocking his shield aside. Lacking protection and with only a sword for defence, he extracted himself too slowly. He did not sidestep quickly enough.

Perhaps he was a split-second too late, having felt, at the instant of piercing the

Cyst's stomach, a violent surge of revenge for his decapitated swornfriend.

Another Reptillian, releasing a double-noted roar at the prospect of a kill, darted towards him with serpent speed, and, in a twist of his wrist, sent a whirling disc towards his prey. It cut into Oschka's sword arm just below the shoulder, leaving the limb to hang by a tendon. Bound in contact by telepathy and discipline, the Keresch leapt to their officer's side. Outnumbered, the remaining Cysts retreated, darting around for robotic mounts. Oschka, rescued by his comrades, was carried on their shields to a healing cave. Our priest-healers worked four days on the maimed warrior. He grew a new arm. He could use it well, but not enough for war.

I will put this story of Oschka into perspective by telling you about our codes of how to keep our emotions in order to reach stability between individuals and our society. The Keresch make bonds of love regardless of sex. Men can take an oath of allegiance with another man or woman. The same options apply to women. Allegiance means fidelity in safeguarding our planet, just as we keep faith with men and women in war and peace, in hardship and ease, pain and pleasure.

Oaths of allegiance can be multiple if desired. To break an oath is paramount to a form of self-destruction. In principle, sworn couples fight alongside each other or back to back: to death if necessary. Yet, regardless of our bravery it does not mean that we have mastered the split between principle and practice. We are not automatons. We have codes of conduct by which a broken oath, a failed contract, is amended through forgiveness, and just as important, restitution. In restitution comes forgiveness witnessed by our tribal community in a short ceremony: the offender kneels before the offended to kiss his or her foot in a gesture of humility. Once the offended has laid a hand of forgiveness on the offender's head, the subject is never mentioned again, ever. Restitution comes with a choice of work or responsibility agreed upon by both parties. It does not need to be connected with the wronged person, but involves some form of community work. Oschka presented himself before the tribal gathering to request his retirement. He wished to be released from his duties as a warrior and join the healers and study their methods. Admittedly, this might have been beyond his ability, not having come from their ancestral line. Without much discussion it was the young Amazon's family who came forward with restitution, by substituting one of their kin to take over Oschka's tribal responsibilities. Deep condolence came from Mynu's family. They admitted sadness at their son's thoughtless rather than disobedient conduct.   It had resulted in his death and his companion's injuries, that, although now  healed, left him incapacitated. Mynu's family offered  to  share  their  home  with him if he  so wished. He accepted with gratitude. He also accepted the stained  banner carried by Mynu before going into battle. Oschka felt proud and  even tingled with pride when the family asked my Commander to entitle him Bannerman.

I now advance in time. Our people being accustomed to a communal loyalty adhered to without oath, on hearing the outcome of our last meeting with the Galactic Council,  we  near  unanimously  decided  to  exile   ourselves.   Withdrawal  was our response to The Crown's cutting reply and supercilious questions regarding our request to share methods of healing agreed upon before battle. Even though the details had not been settled, the principle of an exchange of knowledge between our priests and theirs had  been  accepted  only  in  the  end  to be twisted into a rebuff, a taunt, and almost  an  insult.  Angry  and  disappointed  like superior spoilt brats, we withdrew to lick our emotional   wounds.

At the time, only one amidst our gathering had voiced before the onslaught his quiet disapproval of trying to annihilate the Cysts. He could speak his mind without being asked, not having as yet become a full-fledged priest, keeping to their code of never interfering unless requested or relaying vital information from the Galactic Council. Later it was Bannerman Oschka who became perhaps our most remarkable seer, gifted with wisdom so discreet that it often took us time to appreciate his qualities hidden behind modesty and wry humour.

Although  we  listened  when  he  intimated  that  our ruthlessness might well bring about remorse, we disregarded his comments. We also ignored the cosmic rule of  the  higher  densities  of  seeing  beyond  the  moment  and applying comprehension towards the pain of those living in Darkness. The underlying problem with the Cysts was our inability  to  find  a  solution  to  problems  touching  on  the  complexities of diverse times, spaces and places, and permitting free will in all situations for acquiring the bridge to immortality.

Had not we, ourselves, by free choice after our last war with the Cysts, regressed rather than progressed?

The way to an answer (which anyway would take eons for the Cysts) only came after we had sunk into spiritual torpor. When our time of discomfort came during our self-imposed exile, we saw our transgression and worked to transmute our attitude.

From being warriors engaging in battle with righteous indignation worthy of your St. George forever slaying the dragon, we had to adopt our own form of what your last Buddha called ruthless compassion. It did not exclude using clever persuasion and bargaining for adhering to, for instance, our rules of trade and if we thought necessary even the final threat of outright confrontation. Whatever our methods, we knew at heart that to continue our bellicose brutality in war would win in the short term but not in the long run.

In the past, never having stood by and watched blatant destruction under the banner of freedom of expression for all, due to our rebuff at the Galactic Counsil after the last encounter with the Cysts, we had retreated into indifference for anything outside our own concerns. By grace alone, time brought the balm of the Avatars. They helped us to adjust our way of thinking brought on by the unpleasant event of the doomed lovers.

---

*Thoughtless bravery can be dangerous.*

## CHAPTER 11. THE DOOMED LOVERS

We give a quality to time depending on the purpose of our actions. In our self-exile we became subtly loaded with covert arrogance and obstinacy. The quality of our time was low. Everything we did was second-rate with blunted sensibilities.

Our priests could do little to alter our dulled moods until desire for change came from our hearts, not their lectures. They knew well how ultimately no one can change another, only oneself. Change can be a cloak given by friend or foe, like a garment altering an outward appearance for a time, only to fall into tatters sooner or later if the person does not desire an inner transformation of heart. Like some crystals (or are crystals like us?), we can undergo an inner structural modification covered by an outward appearance that remains the same. Our priests in their patience waited and turned their cosmic eye to the future, creating pathways and openings for Light to enter our psychological gloom.

We continued with our martial training. We studied. We performed our formulas to generate psychic power. We sang and danced as always, perhaps with less exuberance and less discipline that only increased our diminishing state. It lasted for a very long time. During this period, apart from trade, we had little contact outside of our own back yard.

In the round of seasons we harvested our unique dark fire crystals, their value being noble enough for us to haggle with clients on our home ground. When they did not use robots, the big-bellied merchants flew in from all over the Galaxy. Drenched in perfume and self-indulgent finery, they sometimes used these occasions to try and coerce us into battle for their benefit. With repeatedly blunt refusals they learnt that trade, not war, was what we wanted.

"We always knew they were mercenaries!" commented some of the crystal buyers. "All they really want is material wealth. They are now no longer ready to fight for justice, rectitude and the Law of Light… and into the bargain we find them loftily obstinate. Pity!"

With our obstinacy in thinking we could do what we wanted, in a kind of 'do or die' situation, we changed much of our music into a more rigid mode and simpler rhythm. Change the music and you change the mass consciousness. It was to affirm our identity that we, the Keresch, were invincible! What hubris! It was feeding our self-esteem and simultaneously distancing us from our inner core. On two occasions we reverted to a bellicose response after a horde of traders on the outer edge of the Galaxy tried their best to cheat us by stealing more than they paid for. We threatened them with annihilation, Cyst-style. They never returned. The word got out to leave us alone. We were an unrelenting lot.

You might well question why we had immured ourselves in self-righteousness and could not see the dead end of our attitude. Perhaps it was because we justified our position by not hurting anyone but ourselves. 'Ourselves' belonged to us to do with as we pleased. It was like showing others we could behave as we liked. No one had power over us. We had apparently forgotten the loss of power over our lower nature. Only in the more refined consciousness of higher vibration is Galactic Man freed from greed and violence.

We inhabit a realm we term the fourth density, resembling your Buddhist teachings of divisions between lokas and talas, the seven vibrational states of being.

Because all manifestation requires spin and polarity, each state, each level has its lower, denser aspect (loka), and corresponding higher aspect (tala), and our visitors are often beings from frequencies where they are motivated by power.

They still come wanting our warrior blood from our genetic bank in exchange for their extraordinary technology. Rather than trade our genes, we accept the gold in payment for our crystals. It leaves them throwing taunts, and trying to blackmail us with past episodes of our exploits in genome engineering on Earthlings.

"You've put your blooded fingers into pretty little genetic strands!" They say, and ask, "What's stopping you doing it again with us, heh? Why won't you accept far greater payment in cauldrons of gold delivered in Meteor Galleons, far stronger than any of your elegant Sun Ships?"

We refused their currency used for our alchemical purposes rather than coinage. We declined as a matter of personal preference rather than for any righteous moral ground since the idea of their trade no longer appealed to us. We were both obstinate and unpredictable. We could never be brainwashed.

And so it was that by withdrawing from the Galactic Federation, our decline bloomed like an bruised flower in our planet's public eye after an unfortunate incident took place between two of our people from different clans. They broke a most ancient rule of self-awareness acquired through ages of living with an acquired mastery over our lower nature in guiding it to be subservient to the higher, and giving to each its place and function.

Yoneck, a fine young warrior, excellent dancer, storyteller, and student in interdimensional geometric progression, had refrained from making an allegiance with anyone. By no means solitary, he moved in a large circle of friends on all occasions when not bound to his work.

Yoneck probed the mysteries in progressive, interrelated geometric formulas, researched in particular through crystals, and their power to transmit all manner of phenomenafromonedensitytoanotherviaahigherform ofwhatyouknowaselectricity. He worked to harness the signatures of energies permeating our environment and used in teleportation. His beauty of physique and mind attracted a crowd of admirers.

However, his reticence in forming any lasting emotional attachment left friends wondering what impediment of heart and mind motivated such an unusual comportment.

It is true that our lives had become restricted in the use of martial arts during this time of self-exile. In coping with the thieving merchants, we had threatened them just short of using the confrontation inherent in our nature disciplined to employ violence only in battle without emotional attachment.

Perhaps it was this very lack of a physical outlet coupled with the emotional control that had curdled our sensibilities so subtly, yet perniciously enough to corrode our awareness of what was happening. It was first revealed during a sporting match between wrestlers.

The tribes had gathered in our elliptical stadium of tiered amalgamated white stone, its sections hung on overhanging movable ribs adjusted for the desired overall space. In the final round of wrestling the victor, instead of relinquishing his fallen combatant, continued a throttling hold until reluctantly loosened when the spectators began shouting, "Release! Release!" The response was not immediate. Again the crowd cried out, "Enough! Let go!" Finally, only when a master wrestler stepped forward to disengage the couple, did the game end with the victor walking away in a daze, supportively escorted by friends.

"I know how he must have felt," said Yoneck to a companion beside him. "Sometimes, when practicing, I find a dark rage rising up my gullet and I want to strike my opponent in a fury of frustration. I've always been able to master this feeling quickly but lately the emotion has often nearly overtaken me."

He did not talk about his dreams in which he had been unable to stop his KA, previously under the control of his BA, from acts of violence. The KA is bipolar. When asleep, its negative aspect remains to maintain the physical body in its automatic functions, while its positive part, in its vehicle the dark blue KHAIBIT wanders in the realms to which it is attuned. As already mentioned, you can see your own KHAIBIT when you are the Watcher, your Higher Self, observing your astral double in your own dreams.

"Me as well," added another youth. "But I never wanted to mention it. I felt ashamed."

"We should go into the crystal caves with our priests and balance ourselves, don't you think?" said Yoneck.

"Stop worrying!" replied his friend. "It will pass. Don't feed this with your attention; just put more physical strength into your next training. You know how to focus, so don't make problems. There you are studying away at geometric progression, how about putting progression into your attitudes? Don't get stuck, man!"

Previous to our decline, when a Keresch felt their strength failing, they went to the white caves of vast caverns with crystals thick as towering trees growing from dark mineral floors, perfect in their molecular structure to absorb and neutralize destructive influences of a mind out of harmony. Yoneck, like so many others, was filled with prevarication and not inclined to make the journey.

Overheard by one of the more elderly Keresch, a wise-one approaching his 1,500th birthday, he greeted the two young men with a passing smile, and briefly stopped to say: "Young warriors, I see you are beginning to be invaded by weakness. Be careful, please because I foresee coming conflict of a kind you are not prepared for. You see, that soaring brightness of our glorious victory over the Cysts has left a deep shadow equal to the sun's light. You should take a look at it." He passed on straight and slow to join the departing throng of spectators walking along the coloured strip of desert sands on their return home.

My Commander had taken to going alone into the caves to discuss at length with the priests what he sensed was a decline in the general tone of all our people. He was troubled. Nuanced as it was, no one could put a finger on the specific cause of our condition, even if we intuitively knew it stemmed from our collective agreement after the victory over the Cysts. It was as if we refused to review our decision to withdraw after The Crown, in his assumed superiority, had rebuked our Commander in the Council.

Even the reincarnating ancestors, we noted, entered their eggs with greater difficulty and for a greater length of time before birth. An amorphous reluctance hovered in the air, fingering everything we thought and did until, accustomed to the situation, we accepted it as the price to pay for doing what we wanted in exile.

The priests, in their wanderings of consciousness between the many worlds, had been unwilling to tell us more, other than the time was not yet ripe for change. The cause, they told us through our Commander, had to come from us. We ourselves had to bring about the change and the catalyst had not as yet arrived.

We had to sink lower before ascending again towards greater comprehension, coupled with strength gained in overcoming... sloth. They knew this word would offend us when heard at the opportune moment. In their wisdom no priest spoke unless questioned, and if all priests taught, no priest preached.

"Yes!" my Commander said to me. "That is the unacceptable word the priests or I will use very soon to shock us out of reaction into action after an age of self-exile."

Our innate ability for telepathy was another of our characteristics under threat. Few of us heeded the indifference we had attuned to on the broad emotional spectrum of our race. Too many of us wanted to close down and cut ourselves off from negative reception, and beneath most activity of all categories reposed a festering dissatisfaction no one wished to discuss.

Nevertheless, it was witnessed in the combat of the wrestlers and in Yoneck's admission of his own latent fury. It had led him often to wake in the metallic light of pre-dawn and sit upright, holding his kris unsheathed against his chest. He would let his breath out and remain for a minute without air before asking himself, "What is the force I seek?"

One early morning the answer came seemingly from his own voice heard in the middle of his head. "The power lies in your liver. Let your heart rest in gentleness, pass your power to me who directs the force of the kris blade you hold against your flesh."

Yoneck breathed deeply expanding his chest. The gold hilt of his dagger burnt his skin. In that instant a tide of vibrancy entered him, shooting through all 13 chakras from below his feet, up his spine, and above his head, to fall cascading through him in a spout of energy.

"Have no fear!" sang his inner voice. "For I will guard and direct you in invincible strength. You will have what is yours." Yoneck smiled. For the first time he no longer dreaded the heat of all his senses. He would welcome them to clothe his actions. He knew he could at last make allegiance. Who can say if beautiful Yoneck understood what was happening? His education, like all Keresch, included instruction on how to contact his KA in its vehicle, the KHAIBIT, so essential to oversee the material body. On your planet it is usually attracted from a lower dimension from where it ascends for its evolution in the earthly body.

One of our problems at the time of this tale was connected with the lowered frequencies throughout our planet.

Its morphic resonance had brought about a gradually weakened interaction with the *Higher Mind*, and Yoneck fell from an objective, cool indifference into the heat of suppressed passion. In the next ritual in praise of an unusual astronomical configuration, he danced before an audience of thousands assembled in the flat valley between the Crystal Mountains. Projected as usual in a large hologram for all to see, he performed illuminated by the magnetism of inspiration. He danced possessed by his physical energy in a discharge of deep intensity.

Amongst the audience sat a young woman, almost still a girl. Her bright sweetness and delicate build with an abundance of silver-hued hair attracted a horde of friends with the open intent of a possible allegiance. Her name was Yashi.

No Keresch has a family name; a second name of identification is given on merit, in accordance with some notable action or quality observed in the person's development. Oschka was the Mighty Bannerman. Ayesha, our leader renowned throughout the planet, was entitled the True One. I waited to create my name of identification in the future, and in my youthful enthusiasm hoped Ayesha would help me gauge my capabilities and assign me a task in which I would excel.

Returning to the lovely Yashi, her family and my clan had enjoyed a close and long-standing relationship. Ancestors found complicity in returning to continue past affiliations. We proved to be warriors with a compacted strength coming from our fidelities restated over many lifetimes.

At the climax of an astrological configuration auspicious for relationships, we planned the festival for Yashi's first allegiances. Her preference, we took for granted, would be a member from one of our clans. Our bets on her choice consisted of forfeits to be paid in song, dance, or the telling of tales for laughter.

The light had faded by the time an intimate family gathering took place in Yashi's home. From Fire we come. From Fire we absorb our strength. In Fire we forge allegiance. We love a bit of drama and so we awaited her choice, kept secret until this moment.

In a rush of air the flames of cold Fire flared up in middle of our circle of friends sitting in the reception hall hung with living tapestries. Their colour changed like a chameleon's skin adapting to the environment.

The scene was set for allegiance. Schennah, a woman a little older than Yashi, her devoted companion and playmate since childhood, stood north of the fire. Yashi took her place on the south side. They walked through the white flames to clasp hands, and joined by the family Priests and Priestesses, began a chant of vowels taken up by all of us in the strong communal voice of those bearing witness to sacred vows.

Guided by her parents, Yashi's acceptance of Schennah, her childhood playmate, was most fitting. The two young women could grow in knowledge and experience together and deepen their friendship on all levels. Ecstasy of love with man or woman had to wait until a person was at least 100 years of age in your terms or otherwise the frequencies could damage rather than expand consciousness.

On the following morning at the public gathering mandatory for our two clans, Yashi and Schennah walked with the others in double file down the middle of the arena. The music of flutes above intricate drumming pranced its way through the air.

In a wave of spontaneous movement the spectators rose and entered the arena where everyone joined hands to perform the earliest form of group movement known to man. They glided in a circle of increasing velocity until, at its peak, it
broke into two circles whirling in opposite directions before intermingling again.

In the excitement and rhythms holding the pace of the intertwining dancers, on entering the ring Yashi found her hand clasped by Yoneck. Such an innocent and normal gesture should have caused no disruption. Enough to say that in that moment of physical contact of hand and eye the two young people were overcome by a violent attraction for each other. It took their breath away.

Their contact hit both of them in the Swadhisthana Chakra with a force previously never experienced. Unable to take their eyes off each other, Yoneck, pulled along in the circle by the man in front of him, kept his head turned backwards to gaze at Yashi, his face lit by a radiant smile she returned with unabashed acknowledgment.

How do I know all this? Within ten turnings of our planet Yoneck told me detail by detail the course of their entanglement. Caught in a maelstrom of emotion, the young couple broke all rules of protocol. Schennah, devastated from being so abruptly abandoned from any semblance of allegiance, watched Yashi and Yoneck break from the ceremonial dance and rush off together, their escape repeated every evening to secret desert places seldom left before dawn.

Yoneck, consumed in the sudden influx of energy invading his lower chakras, found himself overtaken by the act of sexual mating long transmuted in our race into cosmic ecstasy. Yashi, equally enslaved, thought only of her physical pleasure, its incomparable intensity appearing to be the culmination of all desire. It burnt her whole being with a heat of molten metal.

Our people, soon informed of the liaison, were no more than mildly upset by this unprecedented disregard for all conventions.

"No!" said Yashi, should anyone begin discussing the catastrophe, "I will not forsake Yoneck. My allegiance with Schennah is worthless. My heart has flown to rest in Yoneck's heart. Nothing, nothing, and no one can make me leave him."

"And what of your broken vows? How about the pain you have caused a young woman you loved only a few days ago?" asked her mother.

"No one will punish you," said the family priest, a respected man and Oschka Bannerman's mentor in healing. "But remember you cannot avoid the time when you will review yourself and the gravity of what you are attracting. You can never plead ignorance. You will have to find resolution." Yashi remained silent. She turned and walked away, head erect.

My Commander made no comment in private or public circumstances. The clans wondered why. At the same time, regardless of words or their lack, the result of what had happened sullied frequencies on every level of our environment. Dissatisfaction grew.

Latent violence, reticence to speak out as a group, and the invasion of negative thoughts eroded the previous solidarity of knowing that everyone was connected. No amount of celebrations or games could hide the underlying tension that affected all sentient beings and the milieu of Nature itself. Although we knew what had happened, we could not decide what to do. For a time out of mind no member of our race had reverted to a level where the *KA* had subjugated the higher BA. With us they had worked in tandem, if not always in total harmony.

The *KA*, created at its source as a unit, splits into male and female according to the gender of the physical body into which it is drawn. Here again it splits into two aspects. The negative part remains to regulate all physical requirements leaving, as explained, its positive aspect clothed in its subtle form, to project itself during sleep from the material into the world of dreams.

The *Lower Mind* is often brilliantly intelligent with acute instinct, but lacks that mysterious quality of inspiration and paranormal gift of foresight that taps into fields of information beyond linear time. The brain, a physical organ, resembles a processor, and is affected by the energy of the *KA* that differs from the finer vibrations of the *BA*.

Furthermore the *BA*, in many cultures represented as a bird, is also a unity that splits in entering a body. It too becomes male and female, conforming to the gender of the physical vehicle it joins. You can now see the reason behind the endless search for soulmates, and the confusion between the *KA*, and *BA*, both looking for their other half. A union of the *BA*, the union of true soulmates in your density is very rare. It is too often confused with the *KA's* search for its other half which, if found, causes a near irresistible attraction of two people prepared to cause mayhem in their determination to be together, although when lost in lust their emotional and sexual drive is contrary to the ethics of their higher sensibilities.

Dangerous or not, a strong *KA* is also required to cope with the material conditions of your world and not collapse in the archetype of a gentle poet, succumbing to a consumptive couch at an early age. The other extreme is found in many of your world's ruthless leaders. Take, for example, Julius Caesar with a powerful *KA* in conflict with his awakened *BA* that guided his wise and generous acts. Conversely, in Mozart's Magic flute, Papageno and Papagena are a charming example of the male and female parts of the *KA* happily reuniting into their original oneness.

In your world, certain Muslim teachers interpret the idea of these two principles naming them Qaadem for the Higher Mind and Qaabel for the *Lower Mind*. Spoken of as Angel Guides, each with its own needs, the lower Qaabel must be kept from overruling the higher Qaadem.

The Chinese saw the soul composed of two principles: Kuei and shen. The former, being heavy with the desires of the living, remains near tombs and haunts its old familiar places. The shen is the divine presence within a human being, adding to the perceived dualism of matter and spirit that became transposed into the cosmic balance between the female earthly yin, and the heavenly male yang.

A distinction between what the Chinese named soul (kuei) and spirit (shen) finds similar expression in ancient religions, Greek philosophy (Aristotle, Pythagoras, the Stoics and Plato), and passes on through the Gnostics to St. Paul.
In his first Epistles to the Thessalonians and the Corinthians, St. Paul speaks of what he calls the soul, or psyche, as that which animates the body, while the Breath of Spirit is the part of your immortal being open to the divine, and can illuminate the flesh-bound soul.

Grasp the *KA* principle and you can see more clearly why there are so many extraordinarily talented and brilliant people whose private life is often quite unsuitable to their works of renown. Within each of us these two entities, these two principles, the *KA* and the *BA*, produce friction and contradiction until resolution comes through awareness.

The lovers had been overcome by the attraction of their *KAs*, but our Commander, whenever asked for his opinion on Yoneck and Yashi, made no comment. His face showed no emotion other than interest in the suggestions and questions put before him in our Council Chamber.

Our people had grown lethargic and wanted him to take charge and make decisions they were willing to follow. Knowing the situation he closed the third session saying, "Patience. The fruit is not yet ready to fall. We must allow these two young people time to provoke their own circumstances in which they will find their own solution, painful as it might be. Let each one of us look into ourselves and ask if we have not also of late felt violent and selfish urges come to mind."

Commander Ayesha, terse as usual, made his point without having to elaborate on the theme you Earthlings would describe as pots calling kettles black, when it was ultimately a matter of degree. He knew that a shared intuition would finish his train of thought. The great majority of the Keresch had to put their own house in order before turning on the obsessed couple. They all had in some way contributed to    the troubled psychic atmosphere of the planet.

A rent in the fabric of their auric fields had come about more from their collective sins of omission than anything they had actively done.

Individuals affect the group consciousness and visa versa. The time was near for us to become responsive to our condition or it would spiral down towards us provoking geological upheavals and contaminate our crystals. We had to deal with the root cause, not the symptoms. We swung from the thrust of practically annihilating the Cysts to lapsing into a stationary laissez faire when dealing with our own transgressions. My Commander, in his retreats with the priests, on occasions had gone with them into dream states and perceived the nascent future. His people had fallen from sharpness into bluntness. It would take a catastrophic awakening to prepare them for the coming of the Avatars.

Oblivious to everyone and everything beyond themselves, Yashi and her lover, inseparable and implacable in their intention to remain together, ignored communal responsibilities to the point of insolence.

Studies were dropped, and for the martial arts they went to desert  places. There, in sand behind rocks, they practiced together and lay together for long hours, composing songs in periods of rest.

"It's a form of madness!" commented a close friend after having surreptitiously followed them into the desert. "It's the way those Anunnaki engineered those sex-oriented Earthlings to behave with their warped helix. How that lot progressed is amazing, even if at one point they had the Bridge transferred into  them from other good intentioned Galactics. Remember the wars that that caused?"

Schennah, listening to the group discussing the lovers, felt her skin tingle. "Where is the place in the desert?" she asked.

"Leave them alone," came the reply.

"Why?"

"Because there is nothing you can do. Forget about it," replied another of the friends.

"But it's wrong! My stomach turns and my throat is tight. I feel my heart will break. What's happening," she answered in desperation, "it is wrong and we should call them back and tell them."

Her friends dismissed her opinion. They thought it was a personal matter, not a threat to the community and only of passing interest. Schennah turned away. She left and waited, hidden next to the entrance of Yashi's home.

Dusk fell. Yashi returned to collect a change of clothes and enough nourishment for her immediate needs. Schennah watched and waited. Night arrived before she tracked Yashi far into the desert. She lingered and listened until the lovers were asleep, then scaled the highest rock above their lair and, looking down on their entwined bodies, lay ready for action.

I do not have to know what was in Schennah's mind as she watched the couple deep in shared dreams. It is enough I tell the story from what others and Yoneck recounted in the later trauma of sorrow.

I do know, that like every Keresch when not at study, Schennah carried her kris sheathed in gold. The kris is our emblem. Its history arches back to the Fire Mists before our bodies took on the density of our realm still invisible to you.

She, a group intelligence named Sun Flare, with her heart of flame, Mother-Dreamer of our race, brought into being from the molten proto-metals of our planet, a kris dagger, an object of spiritual import we carry in peace and war.

They hold power in the blades beaten into shape during the folding of our noble metals into and over each other. It gives to the blade patterns, wavy, feathered, or mottled and always of great delicacy.

Near the final stage in making a kris, a further pattern comes when we touch the white-hot blade, pressing it along the edge between our fingers. As with most of our possessions, their making combines thought, rhythm and sound. In forging the

Kris the very pulse of the hammer transmits a fierce energy we know how to produce from ourselves and enhance with our renowned mind technologies.

On your planet there are still ancient peoples who retain the art of enticing a Nature Spirit into an inanimate object, and for as long as it is kept within the     object with incantations and offerings, its power lives. I have watched a shaman using mudra, mantra, and other ingredients to coax an Earth Spirit into a metal statue in an invisible process, unless gifted with second sight.

We, on the other hand, entrap no spirit as such. But with the laws of correspondence, attract and infuse the signature tone at the right pitch and volume of one of our six Elements we feel is best suited to an individual's weapon. It becomes an enriched extension of its owner's power. The small kris, given to a returned ancestor at the end of the welcoming home celebration, is symbolic of the one he or she will receive when physically mature. The dagger must conform in size and proportion to the measurements of its owner's hand, fingers, and forearm.

Yoneck, in his circumscribed and limited bubble of dreams, awoke under a crushing weight on his chest. Within an instant, he caught the raised arm about to stab him. Schennah, having fallen on the lovers from above, emitted a demonic scream. She turned and squirmed, kicked and parried, in a credit to her training in the martial arts. Yoneck, in response, defended himself with a rapidity of movements worthy of a mongoose. The adversaries advanced and retreated in a tension articulated with loud cries of rage, rarely permitted with the Keresch. Indeed they were trained to  keep their emotions in battle on a tight rein, unless sound came  from an outlet of breath energised and concentrated in a force to stun an opponent. Yashi moved alongside the combatants in what she knew was a mortal confrontation. She danced from one foot to the other, prepared to spring with her kris poised in protection of her beloved.

In the darkness of that fatal night Yoneck backed up against a loose stone, and wavered.

In that moment Schennah, screeching like a demented hawk, threw herself towards him, her kris held low to her side. Yashi simultaneously leapt at Schennah, and throwing her off-balance, twisted the weapon from her hand. A split-second later Yashi stabbed her rival, and Schennah, with knees bent, fell onto the dark sand, fast stained with her blood.

Transfixed in a paralysing silence, Yoneck, with his sensibilities numbed and stunned, was in a state of disassociation until it fell away releasing him to face the reality he had, until now, refused to consider.

"Go and hold her!" he commanded Yashi. "Go and hold her. Give her the love you withdrew or her KA will wander in darkness, her KHAT become the vehicle for demons, her BA, pristine in its own realm, will weep. We have, both of us," he continued with hesitation, "committed folly, and not in ignorance."

In silence Yashi wept with her body shaking, and kneeling to cradle the head of her childhood playmate taken in oath of allegiance, she put her forehead to hers, and in a cracked voice murmured, "Forgive me!" Once the mantras and prayers of death had been performed, Yashi and Yoneck lay Schennah's body on the sand, her arms folded with hands holding her kris across her chest. The ritual completed, Yoneck took Yashi's arm. "Come!" He said softly. "We must go now." They held hands for a few steps, then she withdrew, smiled, and went back to where the corpse lay, no more than another shadow on the desert floor. There, standing over the friend she had betrayed, Yashi slowly unsheathed her blood-stained kris. She plunged it into her own heart with lethal swiftness.

Yoneck walked back more alone than he had ever thought possible. He would return with a cortège to take the bodies home for cremation. The shock of death through conflict and anger inundated the collective conscience of the Keresch.
The floodgates of regret opened a tide of disruptive emotion, and we were touched with a guilt rarely felt by our people. The grief beyond suffering and the nagging admission of spiritual irresponsibility coming from negligence opened our hearts for change.

"Change the music," called our Commander at the immense gathering of the clans for the two women's cremation, "and it will begin to heal our society. Today our priests give us their composition in preparation for a transformation. The music," he continued "is a paradigm for us, the Keresch, and in the conjunction of sound and word we will open ourselves again to the emanations focused through our sun. They will touch us all and be reflected back from you in a chorus of recognition. It will," he added in a rising voice, "dissipate your state of... sloth. "The last word alone hit us like a ball on a string returning to its bat.

Let Ayesha's words pull you round a corner of time back into your world. As the deep influence of music expresses, reflects and affects a psychic transformation, a profound change took place in Europe when a single line of melody became polyphonic.

Near 1,000 years later, at the turn of your 19th century, in an era of extreme privilege and poverty in Europe that triggered anarchy and a budding political conscience, Richard Strauss broke the corset of classical composition. He used music as words in describing scenes by sound. It caused an uproar in societies undergoing the threat of innovation. Add to this threat the writings of Frederick Nietzsche, a metaphysical author whose concept of man fulfilling his potential excellence (although soon deformed into dominance by brutality and decadence) inspired Strauss    to compose his famous tone poem, Thus Spake Zarathustra.

These two men, one a brilliant writer, the other a musician, searched for the meaning of existence when you Earthlings were in one of your cyclic struggles of rising from a decaying establishment into a more liberal ethos opposed, and always opposed, by the ancient rule of the Anunnaki elite.

In the long run, my Commander knew that in times of stress the power of music goes deeper than words. Give thought to how, when enveloped by music, we live entirely in the eternal present.

It is time again for Orpheus to play his lyre in the tumult of your present metamorphosis remembering that the perception of music, not confined to one area of the brain, as is memory or sight, touches its whole organism.

After Ayesha's address, many cried out, "Restitution! What can we do for restitution?"

"We have lost the light within," wailed others.
"What's the use of disciplining ourselves with our martial arts, our studies, and artistic creations, when we have lost our way?" exclaimed one woman.

"We have not sunk to the depths of the Cysts!" called out a young boy. "And haven't lied and cheated, why then should we be so ashamed of one incident of violence in times of peace?"

"It's because we have denied ourselves the outlet of war!" shouted another man, followed by the voice of an elder.

"We have not as yet, if you care to think about it, done anything in restitution for the Cysts we annihilated."

"Of course not!" came the response from an elder. "We don't as yet know the art of restoring or healing the beings we fight in the obscurity of their stupidity."

"We need an Avatar for that!" called the unexpected voice of Oschka the Bannerman, inaugurated and now living with the priests. In the following silence Ayesha rose from his chair.

"Unless each and every one of you takes a vow before your family priests that you will sit empty in mind and hearts filled with silence every dawn and dusk until you meet with your Higher Self, you will slowly be swamped by your KA. Until consciousness on our planet is cleansed, we will not attract an Avatar, not at our density, because we should know better and must do better." I felt like adding that we should help ourselves and were not like those on your Earth with splintered psyches and ignorance preserved by your ancient lines of ruling elite. They manipulate the life of your last Christian Avatar into a myth of crucifixion instead of his death being related to the dying and rebirth of the sun deity in a solar cyclic running through your early sacred history. If not physically killed, your great teacher Jesus, a revolutionary you called the Christ, suffered greatly. Have you any idea of the spiritual crucifixion entailed in incarnating in your density?

Your planet is in the middle of 13 realms; counting Earth as number one in both directions, there are six above and six below. You have a unique gambit of creation, a diversity of beings in a polarity of existence that has attracted Galactic interest for millions of years. Fortunatelyyour poles, acting as release valves for the electromagnetic polarity, have saved your planet from blowing itself apart. Maybe I have lived amongst you too often and for too long not to agree with your saying: On the other hand, due to diversity amongst the pigs, you also have pearls of inestimable value. The corpses of Yashi and Schennah, cleansed in the fire of cremation, had released their souls into another existence awaitng reincarnation. It is the same in your world, and in the words of your 18th century Chinese Emperor, Qianlong, the soul's escape via their sacred Mount Tia, seen as a gateway to heaven, is surrounded by the dark seas of space where "dragons (yang) fly and phoenix (yin) dance with powers strange and awesome." Surely the Emperor is alluding to a portal for extraterrestrials to enter by negotiating the electromagnetic surround of your planet.

*"Don't throw pearls before swine".*

The telluric Chinese dragon power, or serpents encircling your globe, are symbols for various forms of energy fields around your Earth. On another level the twisted snakes, so often the emblem of wisdom, in the healers' caduceus, evoke the genetic helix. Your Ancients used metaphor and symbol to describe the quality and functions of forces for which they had no common scientific vocabulary as known today.

They guarded the power of Nature's forces in symbols, often hiding their secret names that they believed if spoken would call forth the action of dangerous powers only controlled by masters. Silence, of course, also included keeping secrets to uphold covert domination as well as a defence against fools.

Unfortunately, due to the trauma of premeditated murder and suicide committed in a state of emotional imbalance, Yashi and Schennah with their consciousness embedded in their *KA*, instead of being liberated from our planet's electromagnetism, were drawn into a vortex, a wailing wind tunnel of grief with blood blinding their eyes.

They were drawn into the habitats of demons and phantoms of the *Lower Mind* so well described in your Tibetan Bardo, a state where the *BA* no longer has contact until conditions prevail for another incarnation. You of Earth have similar tales of Eurydice drawn into an underworld waiting for rescue.

You too after mortal death can undergo another death, temporarily losing your identity in an amorphous no man's land instead of passing into a state of   sovereignty and mindfulness upheld with memory.

You have a choice. We Galactics could well call your world Hades and, as an Irish poet has written: "Light is the only antidote for souls bound to Earth, never forgetting that the higher you rise, the deeper you can fall".
After the women's cremation, following our Commander's suggestion, we turned our warrior discipline into a spiritual discipline. I cannot say if it raised our vibrations in record time, or if it appeared to have come about faster than expected because of our telepathy and our will.

On the other hand, I am prepared to accept that the unmentionable slur of having been called slothful did more than its fair share to spur us on to success.

Be that as it may, in our general newfound vigour and the quickened arrival of incarnating ancestors, we felt it was at last possible to evolve and break out of our old mould. We had regained a strong connection with our Higher Minds. And thus it was that we, the Keresch, waited, watched, and meditated for the coming of an Avatar. We held faith with Light in Darkness. This was a time we had to re-evaluate life and death.

---

*The eternal tale of doomed lovers always includes them doing the wrong thing from the beginning, or the right thing in the wrong way, or the wrong thing based on good intentions that too often pave the road to hell. "OH! Long may the fish-lipped lovers lie kissing catastrophe."*

*Book of Urizen*

*From the depths of dark solitude.*
*From The eternal abode in my holiness;*
*Hidden, set apart in my stern counsels*
*Reserv'd for the days of futurity.*
*I have sought for a joy without pain.*

*William Blake. 1757-1827*

## CHAPTER 12. THE COMING OF THE AVATARS

It was while the priests, my Commander, his five colleagues and myself, together with family and friends, were preparing to recall the shades of the women into the cave, that an unexpected light of unbearable intensity seared our eyes. Perhaps it lasted for but a few seconds, sending us stumbling back against the walls before it subsided into a white and gold glow enfolding two beings. They shimmered, yet remained clear in outline. They appeared simultaneously solid yet transparent. Theirs was a beauty known in our hearts but never seen with our eyes in a splendour barely imagined.

The Avatars had come!

Two *UPS-UNs*, a man and woman united to their BA, had chosen not to manifest as one being, but to stand side-by-side in our density at the very time when we were hoping to bring back two lost souls for help. Our Avatars were no false angels of light who appear in your world to lure the unwary into traps of control during the process of death. I felt my heart would erupt and my body vibrated in a near- frightening intensity. Each of us in the depths of our skull heard the Avatars' message according to our individual capacity to absorb their information. Entire concepts within folds of meaning entered our minds and were infused into our cave's library of great crystal orbs. These two icons of wisdom stood suspended in the air, and in that cave resounding with their communication also transmitted through music, we received their teachings and the nascent future plan waiting to be unveiled.

Announced at dawn throughout the planet, the clans were commanded to gather in the Flat Valley. They came clothed in white, each with tribal emblems marking their chest, their hair clasped in exquisitely-worked metals, a kris at their side, and many with drums slung on their backs. They flew in silently and stepping from their fish- shaped vehicles, flowed with military precision to their customary places beneath the Crystal Mountains, radiating energy into the sky.

A giant hologram stood in the heart of the valley. It showed the raised dais for the priests, and that day it included Bannerman Oschka standing beside Commander Ayesha with his five colleagues.

"Who will wager I am wrong when I tell you the Avatars are coming?" called Bannerman with his arms raised.

He was answered with rolling waves of laughter. His bet remained unchallenged, and in the silence after high mirth with the slow crescendo of drums, our skins tingled. We shivered in an electric tension that filled the air until it split into cascades of glittering particles. They faded, unveiling the Avatars in full glory: enormous, radiant, towering over us with hands outstretched in blessing.

Slowly we knelt in homage. What was transmitted and absorbed by every heart there is a matter of privacy. In whatever form, the teaching came, the presence of the Avatars transmuted us. For some it might have been painful, for others it gave a keystone of understanding, and for us all the experience awakened humility.

We knew as warriors that not only had we to do battle but also to bring Light into Darkness. If we fought in the underworlds and destroyed, then we had also to bring restitution. It was time for some divine meddling.

Who measures time and by what means? Is it by speed, quantity, or quality that we infuse an occasion with unforgettable importance? For how long the Avatars remained towering above us, I cannot say.

Was it in your terms, seconds, minutes, hours, or days? I don't know, just as I cannot gauge the following period when the priests completed what they had begun and called up the presence of Yashi and Schennah to stand before us.

With a part of their psyches lost in darkness, our priests, rather than enter into the density enveloping the women, decided to call them up into a projected manifestation for guidance in our main crystal cave. In this situation we chose not to follow the advanced technology of certain Galactics. We preferred to use our inner power, much of which we knew could not be copied by others unless they were of a higher order.

At present, your misused and over-used technology is becoming an insidious hazard in bombarding your brain and sensibilities with debilitating electromagnetic interference. The electronic gadgets facilitating perpetual communication are at the same time a tracking device, and will be used to control your minds. Should you have the opportunity, you will be astounded at how a good Tibetan, Indian, or Chinese doctor can diagnose the body by pulse, using no instruments other than their five senses trained to expertise over seldom less than seven years.

On the subject of sense and sensibility, one year in Thailand I met a monk with an interesting method of teaching meditation. He interfaced the outer with the inner environment of his pupils by insisting that they choose a sound: for example, bird song, the sound of leaves swept by the gardener, the distant chatter of children, or anything else.

Keeping contact with this sound throughout meditation, the inner and outer realities were looped together, as if passing from one side to the other of a Möbius strip. I return to the technology of the mind that, helped with crystals, we practiced while drawing Schennah and Yashi into the radiant magnetic field created in the main cave.

They stood together wraith-like and near transparent. Their features were blunted in emotional pain and their gestures as slow as their telepathically transmitted words. Each asked forgiveness: forgiveness from each other, from Yoneck, from family, friends, and from the community. "Give us peace of mind and spirit," they begged the priests. "Tell us what restitution we can make. Give us the path to follow. Purify us with Etheric Fire. Give us Light! "To throw shame, blame, and guilt at them was ridiculous.

"I give both of you Love!" cried Yoneck, reaching out towards them. They shimmered and appeared to back away. Love for them at this stage was too much to accept in their grief and self-disgust. They had lost contact with their higher selves and wanted first to be purified, a request the priests quickly performed by bringing forth a circle of flame sent into the area of their apparition. Immediately, their grey forms became a little denser and clearer.

Forgiveness, they knew according to custom, would come after restitution, but what restitution? "It is for you to decide, not us," said the head priest in gentleness. We all knew that restitution is not retribution. Karma is not crime and punishment. It is a way of re-establishing balance and equilibrium.

Yashi bent down to place her forehead on Schennah's foot. She longed to reincarnate soon, and in restitution work in the lower densities helping those like herself who wanted to commit murder and suicide. She chose her task to last for an unspecified time, that in her own assessment would appease her conscience.

She also knew she had to meet Yoneck again in a future life and adjust their relationship. The priests bore witness. Then they asked Yashi to forgive herself.

Until this difficult task was achieved she would not be emotionally free from her folly of willfully disregarding what she had known would hinder her evolution and cause pain to others. Schennah, in comparison, who had been murdered before she could murder, was in a state of confusion. She craved forgiveness from Yoneck and accepted his love with less reticence than had Yashi.

All the same, when asked to forgive herself, her form grew cloudy, streaked black as if with blood, and her thoughts were immured in self-loathing. It took time and energy for the priests to remain in contact with her. Schennah could absorb a little of everyone's forgiveness, but could give herself neither love nor pardon. After an aching dialogue, she finally decided on her restitution. Under the circumstances it was    not surprising that she decided to become an exile from our planet, wandering the Galaxy without asking protective allegiance from anyone.

She chose to work in the most humble way as an underling, learning to regain on another level her courage as a Keresch warrior. Her choice was bravery itself, induced to overcome the damage done to all those she had thoughtlessly harmed. If the women silently asked for immediate grace coming from universal love, so mysteriously granted when appropriate, I do not know. They could not claim ignorance, and through the restitution they had chosen, they would experience, remember, and add substance to their being by transmuting dross into gold.

Otherwise, the human entity could be similar to an onion and its many skins which, when removed, leave no essence enriched by experience. One could say you would remain like disincarnate beings with no memory, no crystalline psychic core amalgamated into existence through a host of experience.

Perhaps this is why some angels bow before the endurance and faith of you Earthlings.

The two women, bound to each other by mutual consent, requested to incarnate as soon as possible. In the state where they were temporarily disconnected from the BA's Higher Consciousness, they waited and would prepare for their next physical embodiment as errant Keresch. Yoneck, after receiving forgiveness from those he had wounded, requested to begin immediately on a mission to your planet. Little did he know what he was in for! He was confident he could, in his wanderings, adapt himself to spend long periods teaching physics with ethics in a society increasingly involved with domination. Ayesha laughed heartily.

Love. Loss. Repentance. Restitution. Resolution. Like basic colours limited to what your eyes can register, they repeat themselves in the tales of love retold and reenacted over the ages of your existence. Are there new scenarios for love and death, pain and pleasure, in the dramas played out in the proverbial theatre of life? Could Yashi and Yoneck, Romeo and Juliet, or Abelard and Héloïse have avoided their tragic fate?

The most frustrating aspect in the roles you Earthlings play, is about not remembering what you may have learnt, hence avoiding the same mistakes made more than once in more than one incarnation. Is this repetition perhaps because you do not pay attention to the presence of the present in your thoughts and actions? Look at any painful situation, specifically in the case of doomed lovers and the effects of their actions on others, and surely, in the words of your deeply thoughtful writer C.S. Lewis, one of the miracles of love is in the power it gives in seeing through its own enchantment and yet not being disenchanted.

Keep this in mind and use it as a stepping-stone when, out of despair spawned by acute distress, you forget the compounds of what you are. Abelard, in experiencing his pain, cried out:

> *... the love of God in its beginning does not wholly annihilate the love of the creature*

He had not resolved the conflict between the *KA* and the *BA*.

---

> *We can rise with our own fortitude in adversity by first emptying the mind,*
> *giving as some Muslims say, space for Allah to move.*
> *Look for light and simplicity rather than a perpetual dialogue with self.*

*Black as the devil, hot as hell, pure as an angel, sweet as love.*

*Charles Maurice de Talleyrand 1754-1838*

*Proverb*

*To everyone is given the key to heaven;*
*The same key opens the gates of hell.*

## CHAPTER 13. ATLANTIS

This was the background for our decision to come again  on to your Earth. We were, believe it or not, in a certain sense naïve. In another age we had worked with interdimensional Galactics in transmitting to Earthlings under our care the Bridge, with part of your body's genetic coding taken from Star People's extraterrestrial essence. Its infusion into your race would awaken the pituitary and pineal glands so vital in the subtle connection between  the  intangibles  of perception, thought, and emotion deciphered through the  brain.

The greater the awareness and contact with the psychic constitution, the quicker it can affect genetic structure.

Since at certain times this relationship with the Anunnaki scientists had proved that not all of them were tarred with the same brush, we thought they would accept us at face value. Ayesha, Yoneck, and myself, accompanied by other Keresch, arrived on one ship landing in the north-east of the main island of Atlantis.

I recall only too well the effect of walking out into your planet's atmosphere. It was as if my heart, lungs, and muscles were collapsing under an unbearable density. My head felt pressure from without and within, and I sat quietly on the ground beyond our ship's field of influence, adjusting to this new environment. It took time to master until we could manage prolonged periods without discomfort.

Picture in your mind Atlantis: a beautiful land, a continent with an archipelago of southern islands already separated by cataclysms.

Like stepping-stones they gave access to colonies in South America, and for thousands of years a great network of trade flourished from the shores of Antarctica to outposts in north, west and southern Africa (for gold, Egypt, the Middle East, India, and Asia. It is not my intention to give a detailed story of Atlantis, only an account of my time on the main island of this empire.

Having been asked to establish a birth complex, we set it in a landscape of hills green with cereals turned to undulating gold in autumn. We designed a circular building, a rotunda of leaping arches under a wide dome of alabaster, with a ball of crystal covering the circular opening in the roof.

The Rotunda housed space for teaching and monitoring pregnant women. We also gave courses in every aspect of infant and child-care, attended by men and women of all ages interested in the process of foetal development from conception to delivery.

Some intimate chambers had glass clear pools where dolphins, so similar to mankind, although different, waited telepathically, ready to aid birth given in water.

They added to the Rotunda's ideal environment for the incoming child.

Experts in our advice of sound and colour, we used convivial frequencies to help the minds and bodies of the mother and their offspring, as well as parents in pre- and antenatal care. We worked with the Anunnaki. They put no restraints on our research. They agreed to let us improve the process of birth. They encouraged us to monitor traits in humans with unusual intelligence combined with clairvoyant aptitudes and artistic abilities. They claimed they wanted humans endowed with the logic of physics, the imagination of artists, and the foresight of psychics, planted in a strong and beautiful physical vehicle. They let us construct our own laboratories for our mind-medicine. We knew how genetic data, apart from the environment, stress, and diet, could be modified by elevated thought and emotion filtered through the pineal and the pituitary glands.

As at this stage of your development, the faculty of imagining an experience was less clear, less full and less strong than it is in your era; we used holographic images for virtual practice. It gave a better understanding of how a mother could have an effect on the emotional state and physical appearance of her offspring when still in the womb. It was a work of joy and laughter. The children born during our time there were more advanced than their predecessors.

126

Ayesha, pleased with our results, left me to continue with the support of our Keresch colleagues and the daily presence of Yoneck. From wandering Atlantis as an observer and teacher, he had become a permanent member of our team, and, as an expert in monitoring frequencies, continued his work on multidimensional geometrics. In both work and play he was an enchanting presence, entertaining us with songs both traditional and of his own invention. His was the balance between musician, dancer, and scientist. Beautiful as the dawn with a mind honed sharp as a laser after his lapse into the blindness of passion and the death of two women enmeshed in his destructive triangle, he still retained an irresistible charm.

We all loved him.

Whenever he danced for entertainment, the two of us exchanged knowing looks in reminiscence of the days when he had first beguiled young Yashi. I wondered how he had tamed his inner fires, that now apparently mastered, left him to concentrate on his work with an overview of making amends as fast as possible for his past actions. One late afternoon Yoneck sent me an unusually curious and intelligent mother. After the birth of twin boys she had requested to become part of our team.

She collected data in practical ways by gathering information from her people in a non-intrusive approach, and already had helped care for the young, returning for further education with their parents. Her name was Manisa, the Sweet One.

After noting the absence of her twins, I asked where they were and why we had not seen them or a few of the other young children at the Rotunda. She glanced into the distance before answering with lowered head. "They have gone with their aunt to see their grandmother on the south island. Grandmother went there some time ago to claim new land in what she thinks is a better climate for old people and has a more reliable governance in the distribution of crystal power. It is used there, I believe, with much more openness and benefit for the people than here. You know how here it falls under the control of our Principal Commission."

She could not say when the children would return. I saw fear hidden in her irises. I felt fear fastened to her heart. This was neither the time nor place to ask further questions, so I watched Manisa stand in silence, knowing well how much this woman needed my support in a scenario she could not reveal. I walked a few paces from her before an urge made me turn. Looking back into her face, I was filled with perplexity. I had seen in her eyes the glow of a pleading need I could not return.

This was the period when I unwittingly passed from Light into Darkness, a profound darkness that remained for so long, and hovered over me like a thin shadow of menace, retaining in its presence the memory of that distant Atlantean nightmare about to happen.

Shortly after my encounter with Manisa, one opalescent evening, on leaving our arched and domed Rotunda, I saw an Anunnaki previously unnoticed suddenly disappear. He walked towards an incline on the nearest hill covered with the ripening corn and sank into the ground.

I followed at a distance until I came to an unobtrusive hollow with a narrow tunnel. It had, curiously, no door. I waited trying to discern if there were any invisible barriers to this opening. Instinctively, I projected my awareness to test the situation, and found nothing to prevent my entry.

On guard I went in, bending to pass a good hundred metres along the dank passage running deep into the earth. Coming to a large, equally-dim opening with a frequency obstruction, unable to continue I stood there, my head lowered, and felt vulnerable without my kris. At this point my memory holds the feeling of being enveloped in a suffocating and overwhelming presence. Flushes of hot and cold fear rush though my body. I feel sapped of all alertness.

---

A brilliant light flashes on. I am blinded as three Anunnaki swiftly paralyse my body and try to dull my mind. I am dragged into a great chamber. I cannot name the unusual smell. Huge transparent vats stand in rows. They are filled with the bodies of Earthlings. My captors, knowing I was still conscious, take an insane pleasure in showing me the numerous genetic manipulations they have achieved with varying success. The results are terrible. Although virtually immobile, my eyes still focus and I register with horror the monstrous experiments the Anunnaki are making in the name of genetic possibilities. Bat-like humanoids lie next to human foetuses. Deformed humans appear to be in hibernation with faces emerging from the plasma sustaining their bodies. Tanks hold dismembered limbs and body parts for testing the cells' capacity to grow with the influx of Etheric currents. Human and animal embryos are only too recognisable in the dimness slashed by changing spotlights, illuminating the Anunnaki researchers in their investigations.

A low, invasive hum fills the laboratory. I am dragged further into the chamber. There, to my right, are transparent coffins under Anunnaki surveillance with a few dazed Earthlings.

Dressed in grey uniforms, the latter, their eyes dull, tend to the life- support systems of stolen humans. Most of them are children.
In the rows of transparent coffins I see the twins lying immobile, their eyes open and unfocussed in their expressionless little faces.

I instantly understand what is happening to them. Born under our enhanced conditions and genetic improvements, they are abducted, brought into the underground laboratory for experiments. When taken over by the Anunnaki, they become mind-controlled, possessed by one of them attempting to claim the child's incipient Higher Mind as its own by proxy. My physical condition has rendered me helpless, if not quite devoid of my senses, until I am further incapacitated. Put in a chair, my head is prepared for intrusion and the rape of my knowledge.

Strange how the essence of one's being still sparks in the pits of despair. "I am Light!" I cry in silence. "I am Light. Light will prevail." I know they will cleave my *KA*, leaving only its lower half to keep my body barely alive.

Then comes oblivion. I remember nothing after my final psychic violation that leaves me dysfunctional, lying encased in a glass-like sarcophagus. Rather than be bound to this event in memory, emotion, and sensation, I use it to install an objective vigilance, a weapon against forgetfulness; for unless I remember the end of this experience I am held captive to its forgotten conclusion, and hold sentiments of abandonment. I have no recollection of how I escape from the underground laboratory.

Did I walk through walls? Hardly possible in the state I was, with half my *KA* captured and distorted, its other half still with me maimed to within an inch of my body's life, and any connection with my *BA* fried to a crisp. Perhaps some secret sympathiser smuggled me out: I have not as yet steeled myself to hunt for the truth. Although I am a Keresch I hide behind the excuse of waiting for time to offer me the answer. I call myself a coward. Why will I not search for the person that saved me?

All I can bring to mind is how I later wandered as a sand-beggar through villages receiving alms in my outstretched hands and giving in return archaic words of gratitude.

They fall like hot pebbles from my slobbering lips. Resembling a lemming I make my way to the sea, and there on the shore in the soft sand I draw with my fingers, desperately trying to join the lines of a three-sided geometric shape. I know I have to send a message home through a triangle of flame. The ship comes. I am carried aboard and die from my body held by my Commander, his forehead pressed to mine. I pass through his mind in an immense wave of power and protection. I spin through a vortex to regain full consciousness in the calm of the density where I will reside until my next incarnation. I know at the moment when the silver cord of my maimed *KA* broke, Ayesha disintegrated its sheath back into the elements, beyond the grasp of the Dark Ones in that subterranean Atlantean crypt of Death.

Why had he deserted me?

---

*Why indeed, and is this the truth?*

*Long is the way and hard, that out of hell leads up to light.*

*John Milton 1608-1674*

*Cry "Havoc!" and let slip the dogs of war.*

*Shakespeare 1564-1616*

## CHAPTER 14. RETURN AND THE ART OF WAR

One evening, in my next incarnation on my planet, warmed in the light of our sun sinking behind the Crystal Mountains emitting their spectrum of light into the darkening sky, I sat with my Commander in his home overlooking the valley. Of late we had all been uneasy with tinges of foreboding. Ayesha was troubled and wanted to consult the priests. Our reminiscing of the last battle with the Cysts proved to be no coincidence when Bannerman arrived unannounced.

He entered dressed in the pale blue robes of his position as healer and assistant priest. He joined our flow of conversation in perfect accord and waited for Ayesha to speak.

"Beyond this chat, what brings you here dear Bannerman? Confirm my thoughts."

"In verity I will confirm your perceptions. We have received communication from the Galactic Council today. The Crown is sending his... or is it her? I forget... private secretary to speak with us tomorrow. More was not transmitted."

"No need," replied Ayesha, always somewhat brief in reply. "Haven't we just been talking about the Cysts?"

Next evening in an assembly of all the Keresch tribal leaders, the usual hologram in the valley relayed the event throughout the planet. No explanations were needed, only a few details and an accord to be signed and witnessed. The Crown's secretary, an overwhelming matriarch of considerable ability, opened the gathering with the briefest of protocol saying, "As you have surmised, the Cysts are preparing to attack your planet and destroy every life form it nurtures. Our intelligence confirms this. Knowing your reticence to join our Council or any intergalactic conference, we nonetheless wish you to accept our support immediately in this potentially very dangerous situation. We have just one question. Do you agree?"

It may seem strange when I tell you of our response. No Keresch moved a muscle. No noise entered the air. A silence, vibrant with positive power, absorbed everyone. Every thought had become transmuted by agreement into a living force field that enveloped the planet. It overrode any need for words of affirmation. We, the Keresch, were ready.

"Send me your warriors as soon as possible," said the Secretary. "We will meet in The Crown's Green Hall as usual for our plans of protection, and also, I am sure, plans of attack."

We had four days to prepare. On the last evening the whole horde of us gathered to dance, this time not for entertainment but as a rite before battle. From birth we train to have equilibrium of mind and body and to master our fiery and impulsive natures. The arts of self-control and martial movements teach confidence that we exhibit in magnificent ritual presentations composed of great numbers of people. Dance is the other side of martial training, and our performances express marriage between art and science. They release an extraordinary, almost tangible energy. That night, lit by high flame, we danced in groups to the beat of drums under string and wind instruments. If you have seen your Sikhs move in their martial arts, wielding their long double- handed swords, then you have an idea of the swiftness of our movements in entertainment and war. The warrior dances and rhythms found in the peoples of your Middle East, Balkans, and Caucasus are reminiscent of our ethnic expressions. We sing too, the voices of our women soaring like flutes in open or closed harmonies.

Our men love polyphonic song as well as a type of plainchant, originally coming to your planet when Atlantis was in its full glory, and each dance is accompanied with its appropriate musical scale and rhythm. A fair number of our dances are based on the celestial movements in our planetary systems, or represent the intermingling of geometric shapes inherent in our Elements.

At this point I must add some interesting information. As you know we, the

Keresch, were present much later at different times in the land you call China. We helped perfect their martial arts and strategy attributed to a certain Sun Tzu whose date of birth, reputed to have been around 400 BC, is secondary because it was our knowledge transmitted over time that taught them the manoeuvres of war.

The importance of what they learnt from us and applied to their own culture is to this day still valid for battle or politics, and the discipline of good governance. It is an impressive collection of balanced insights stating, as we know: war is based on deception. Accordingly, in fighting the Cysts, we would once more hold to our knowledge of combat that later, eons in the future, we gave to Sun Tzu, this Chinese master of strategy.

> *When these five kinds of spy are all at work, none can discover the*
> *secret system. This is called "divine manipulation of the threads." It is*
> *the sovereign's most precious faculty.*

Although we knew, as well as most, how news in the Galaxy is seldom ignored, in our self-exile we had withdrawn from normal communication between star systems. Others might know about us. We, by choice, did not in turn know much about them. They knew about our encounter with the Avatars but not what we might do in battle after this experience. As for us, we could not gauge our ability never having put the Avatars' teaching into practice during war. Learning is one thing, to absorb and use it in diverse circumstances demands time.

The opportunity to discover the difference between theory and application had come none too soon. No sophisticated technology of contingency could simulate what our emotions might be under the pressure of war. We had not tested or been tested. To begin with, on this occasion we could offer no information from our spies. We had none. The Galactic Federation would surely cover our ignorance with their own information about the Cysts.

Ayesha, his five companions, and me, entered the Green Hall to stand in front of The Crown. The title remained, the person occupying the position had changed from our last meeting. We faced a small, round, bright-eyed being, perhaps man or woman, with a wide aura of beautiful graciousness and wit. The inspiring charisma of this Crown's presence touched us with a smiling devotion equally felt in the assembly of the Galactic Armed Forces composed of a multitude of men and women from star systems acquainted with the Cysts. They had come to join and coordinate the confrontation with our enemy, the humanoid reptilian predators.

*He will win who has military capacity and is not interfered with by the sovereign.*

All of us thanked the The crown for permitting us, the combined forces, to have a free hand in our strategies.

*In respect of military method, we have, firstly, Measurement; secondly, Estimation of quantity; thirdly, Calculation; fourthly, Balancing of chances; fifthly, Victory. Fighting with a large army under your command is nowise different from fighting with a small one: it is merely a question of instituting signs and signals.*

With a surprising lack of complications, the representatives of the diverse host of warriors commanding gigantic mother crafts and hordes of fighter capsules coordinated their plans in record time. Intelligence had relayed the Cysts' strategy. They planned to encircle our planet in stealth by remaining in an invisible frequency for as long as possible. No new trick for us, but this time evidently they would come with over five million fighters, including robots and newly invented weapons of death.

We too could muster near two million Keresch warriors from our limited population on our small planet, although it would tax our social structure should the battle last too long. We were also warned that our technology was not up to standard. We needed extra shielding to avoid contamination. It was optimum to engage the

Cysts in space rather than on our home ground, and stay clear of mortal combat in the old style. In a deliberately slow movement Commander Ayesha stood up, and with an expression of amusement said:

"My esteemed colleagues, I am sure you remember what we, the Keresch, teach our warriors. If you know yourself, you need not fear the result of a hundred battles. If you know yourself but not the enemy, for every victory you will also suffer a defeat. If you know neither you will succumb in every battle. No need to add that we all know the enemy and hopefully ourselves." We were, each of us, as expected, animated by the same spirit.

I now write words, recorded far in the future by Sun Tzu, a time traveller but voiced that day by Ayesha in our council:

> *Which of the two sovereigns is imbued with the Moral Law? Which of the two generals has most ability? With whom lie the advantages derived from Heaven and Earth?*
>
> *On which side is discipline most rigorously enforced? Which army is stronger? On which side are officers and men more highly trained? In which army is there the greater constancy both in reward and punishment?*

Polarities were about to clash. Two military forces from different realms were at war. Which indeed would prove the stronger in the advantages of Heaven or Earth? Discipline was equal. The character of the fighter was different. Rewards were equal in granting what each side considered the prize: power, booty, and loot, or Light and law? The query brought snorts from everyone.

During our conference, in the times of relaxation and convivial talk with the many Galactic races, a bounteous array of different physical types, I smiled and recalled how we always said:

*The expenditure at home and at the front, including entertainment of guests ..how we, the Keresch, always said.*

It was and always is a matter of balancing what is given, no matter the cost, with the gain most likely to be obtained. We had already learnt a lot from mingling with the Galactic Forces. Although untrained in our methods, they could follow what we could accomplish by mixing mind with matter. On the other hand they were proficient with extraordinary technical devices and also affiliated with mental activity in a different way.

*Security against defeat implies defensive tactics; ability to defeat the enemy means taking the offensive. The general who is skilled in defence hides in the most secret recesses of the Earth; he who is skilled in attack flashes forth from the topmost heights of heaven. Thus, on the one hand we have ability to protect ourselves; on the other, a victory that is complete.*

In short, our preparations required flexibility (a rare attribute in the Cysts) and instantaneous synchronization via holograms in every ship, showing the positioning of our combined fleet. We decided to create a circular corridor of protection lying between two shields around our planet with a subtle opening luring in the enemy. We have long held this strategy in various guises.

*When an invading force crosses a river in its onward march, do not advance to meet it in mid-stream. It will be best to let half the army get across and then deliver your attack.*

The main strategy was to find the enemy's Command Galleon, obviously with its escort vessels, let them break through our outer defence, then dispatch fast attack ships of our combined forces to encircle and capture this spearhead of the Cysts. We would use our swarming technique, herd the flagship into a position to our benefit, and, with their leaders in our hands, we could have the advantage. Our basic plan we knew would have variations according to the opponent's tactics.

*Therefore, just as water retains no constant shape, so in warfare there are no constant conditions.*

Contingency plans were agreed upon. Watchword transposed into an extraordinary glyph was our password. What would be our decisive weapon? No one had a precise answer until Bannerman the Seer came through on the central hologram. He stood there, his hands enfolded in his pale blue sleeves, the tip of his wispy mandarin beard tickling his chest emblazoned with a cross section of a great, dark, reddish mauve fire crystal. He bowed, slightly smiling, with eyes narrowed in keen observation, and then with chin raised he spoke.

"Greetings! Permit me, my colleagues, to offer you a very simple suggestion, perhaps too simple, or perhaps too intricate to apply. Two events came to mind, one past and one in the future."

Seer Bannerman in his easy amused tone of voice described the experience of being flooded in the radiance of the Avatars' near-unbearable light, nonetheless adjusted to our embodiment. "I then, at one time, looked into the future possibilities and came, yes, by accident perhaps, to the planet Earth I know you are acquainted with. What I beheld was primitive and very effective. The Earthlings had long lost the great empire of Atlantis and were warring amongst themselves for supremacy." Bannerman paused before continuing.

"I became intrigued by what was happening in the eastern part of what would be known as the lands of the Mediterranean. What I observed were a people called the Romans, a bellicose, practical lot, makers of law, engineers somewhat sterile in imagination but with a disciplined army and an aim to expand their territories. They were having a war with another culture and race called Greeks. The obstreperous, unruly Greeks, a strange mixture of fighting men and artists, architects and abstract thinkers, were at best inventors of new theories. They excelled as scientists and mathematicians searching for the reason behind phenomena. They were a strange gathering of Anunnaki and Galactic heritage.

"I watched the life of an unusual Greek nobleman, son of an astronomer, a mathematician, and inventor named Archimedes. His was a Galactic intelligence that divined formulas of calculation way beyond his time. His social graces were few because he lived in his own world of calculations and geometry. Socially, he was unfortunately clumsy.

Among the most useful of his inventions was a certain type of screw, named for him. He further demonstrated mathematically the deceptively powerful and simple use of the lever. He then became overexcited upon calculating the exact displacement of water when any body was put into a tub, his own in particular. "I have it!" he cried in jubilation, and climbing out of the water dashed into the street, clad only in a small towel. He calculated Pi, and also constructed parabolic mirrors with which he blinded the sailors and set aflame one Roman ship in the fleet invading his port.

"This is where, delighted as a child, I made the connection of Light being used for our purpose. Now! May I suggest we use not mirrors but light in its purest form from space and adjusted in quality and quantity to stun the Cysts? Their constitution cannot stand this form of Light. We don't have to use it at a disintegrating strength, just a subtle level of light administered in a dosage beyond their capability to cope with."

"Bannerman! Are you suggesting we use a light like the radiance of the Avatars?" asked one of the physicist engineers.

"Put it like that, yes," said Bannerman. "Simulate the frequencies. It will be virtual of course. We cannot duplicate the emanations of an Avatar. Otherwise, you will have to request the genuine thing. Up to you!"

This was my time to rise. "Esteemed Bannerman," I began, "why have you not suggested what is the obvious?"

The council looked on attentively, vaguely perplexed. "Because, collectively, if we, the Keresch, add the powerful use of our minds enlightened with the Light of the Avatars, plus the Light induced by technology, this will carry an astounding impact. Every Galactic involved can join his own energy to this equation."

The gathering saw the point. It was a solution in the name of Cosmic Mind. As an armed force of many races we were over seven million strong with confidence in our mission. We had reached a concordance of intention and understanding. Strengthened by telepathy, our solution to defeat the Cysts worked like an electric current running through the minds of our leaders. Words were almost unnecessary. The detailed choice of tactics would present itself during battle. We were sure our communications would withstand the Cysts' up-till-now unsuccessful efforts to break our codes.

Their most formidable weapon was the use of energy that could immobilise us more than our technology. If you think of insects passively obeying a group consciousness, ours was wrought into a collective consciousness created by us, and it obeyed us, not the other way round. We were entering war with a species of humanoid life, our polar opposites as it were, and against whom we needed to protect ourselves without losing sight of them being part of sentient creation that regrettably threatened our existence.

All manifestation comes from unity, and in your terms, over a mind-numbing span of time everything returns to the source of unity.

There is a place for Light and Darkness on every vibrational level of our universe in which consciousness can expand or retract in experience. Difference occurs in the descent of vibrations entering heavier densities with greater polarities from where consciousness can expand or contract. Our world has had its galactic connections in a universe that is around fourteen billion years old. In the Milky Way alone, many extraterrestrial civilizations exist, some as physical as yours, leaving others invisible to your mortal eyes. At the time of our preparation for our great war with the Cysts, we were joined mainly by the Pleiadians, assisted by the dark skinned Sirians, and a few from the Orion constellation who held the Light from having mastered polarity, regardless of the perpetual wars waged in that star system. The latter were representatives of an integrated consciousness that sent its emissaries to watch over our confrontation.

*Remember you have made contracts consciously and unconsciously in a myriad of times and dimensions forgetting your existence as a soul beyond the confines of your body. Choose well those with whom you co-create.*

*In the silence of space our hearts held the thunder of war recalling that sometimes the vanquished have as much glory as the victor.*

*Keresch Chronicles of Conflict*

## CHAPTER 15. THE GREAT CYST WAR

The Galactic Forces, as decided, created a protective ring in outer space. Within it, we, the Keresch, formed a second inner ring using the forces around our planet. We planned to herd the enemy's Flag Galleon through a hidden opening into the corridor between the rings. We knew they, like us, could warp space, but we had our antidotes.

Between the two circles we had the corridor filled with our combined ships waiting to apply our tactics. We were following our metaphor of using the powers of Heaven and Earth in our double circles. We let the Galactics fight the invaders in a furious battle above the outer ring. They cunningly drew the Cysts' formation away from their central Battle Galleon and its escorts, which with a sudden gap in their formation, we attacked, and forcing the cornered enemy to pass into the corridor between the outer and inner circles, we closed the opening defended by our allies.

Once the Galactic Armada, filling the dome of the sky in a fearsome silence of power, had herded the enemy into the corridor, our attack fleets lowered their vibration and became visible. Greater in number and more than a match for the Cysts, they flew alongside the invading cortège and set in operation a wavelength that disrupted its weapons for retaliation. We then swarmed the flagship like bees with myriads of small whirling discs forming an impenetrable shield. Nothing could get in or out of the swarm field except our own devices. They included projecting an insufferably high-pitched hum into their control room.

The Cysts 'command vessel was blocked from further movement, and, holding their emperor, the awesome Thisixt and his staff, they soon became our captives.

Then, in typical if unnecessary bravura, we confronted the emperor with an over-large hologram of our leaders headed by Ayesha. In a quiet voice he unilaterally threatened our prize prisoners with total annihilation, despite this method having been forbidden by the Galactic Federation.

At first they laughed, replying that such tactics would destroy us as well as them since they knew how to return the force. We held firm. The Scorpion, we replied, was prepared to sting the enemy on his back even if it killed himself in the process … such was our nature! Surely the great Thisixt knew this? We, the Keresch, convinced our enemy of our threat. It was pure bluff.

Had we not always found that the art of war is primarily based on deception? Once the captives were transported to our vast Command Galleon hovering above the Crystal Mountains, we offered the emperor and his entourage repentance not annihilation, providing they changed their ways. Otherwise, a different fate awaited them.

They and their cohorts were to be returned and bound to the lower realms to continue their onslaughts of destruction. Well versed in the Cysts' tactics of compliance broken at the earliest opportunity, we were on guard for fraud, yet gave fair measure for a change in heart. We knew it was useless to extend this choice to the whole Armada of our enemy, even if the order to obey us was given by their emperor; it would be but a sham for escape. The arrested battle remained only for as long as we had our captives. The potency of our plan depended on secrecy and timing.

Seven of our priests and seventy-seven others were on board, representing the wisdom of our Galactic allies. As non-combatants and observers, they would facilitate negotiations if necessary. Although we had reached a checkmate and the whole of the Cysts' Amarda knew about our prized hostages, it was still a fluid situation where, stationary above our home planet, anything could happen should the defence ships around us be drawn off, and frequencies changed in disorienting space warps. And happen it did when, the seventy-seven wise beings came forward in a tight line to face our Cyst prisoners. In silence they looked into the eyes of these reptilian humanoids. They gazed at them without judgment, leaving room only for the hostages to assess themselves, and possibly accept the choice before them. They were told that they could, if desired, change the direction of their evolution.

Thisixt, the paramount Emperor, arose erect in his hideous majesty. His yellow eyes darted from face to face in the solid phalanx of men and women in front of him. His entourage stood behind with bowed heads, waiting. Ayesha spoke in an almost disinterested voice. "As High Representative on my planet you come to destroy, I now offer clemency to you, the Emperor Thisixt and your captive Cysts on this ship. The choice must be quick, and, notwithstanding your choice, the rest of your kind will suffer. Remain with them or change your path. The decision is yours."

What did we expect? What could we expect? What did we want for ourselves? What did we want for the Cysts?

As the mighty emperor crumpled on his knees with a strangely unnerving high pig-shrill squeal, his entourage knelt behind him hissing like geysers with heads touching the floor and arms crossed over the back of their necks.

The hall stank with the release of their fear as their leader pleaded to be killed. He knew that to be slain without hatred or revenge but with blessings that would release him from his body, he would be guided to a region less dense than his home planet. From there he could begin ascension into Light, quickly or slowly according to his will and intent. He, like his fellow captives, could with our blessings become an extraordinarily clever KA, waiting to be tamed in a human incarnation. With the example of their leader, the other Cysts followed suit. First came the ritualistic death performed by our priests.

They laid a sword of transmuted gold on the neck of each hostage, quickly followed by execution with a painless ray. Ally and foe instantly knew what was happening. All Hell, or if you wish all Heaven, then broke loose in an overwhelming thunder of Light and chant from millions of Galactics in the tongue of the Multiverse. The exorcism had begun. It is an extraordinary remnant of timeless knowledge transmitted in universal and cosmic metaphor beyond the chains of your Catholic church. How it has survived in such simplicity is a miracle. It is as potent as any rite of expulsion, especially when amplified with our Light, the right pitch, volume, and sound, and chanted in the Esperanto Galactic tongue:

*"By the seven gold candlesticks, and by He who is like unto the Son of Source standing in the midst of the candlesticks; by His voice, as the voice of many waters; by His words, I am living, who was dead; and behold, I live forever and ever; and I have the keys of death and of Hell. I say unto you, creatures of perdition: depart, depart, DEPART!"(\*)*

We, the Keresch, had been marked by the presence of the Avatars. They had touched us in the quintessence of our being. What we experienced during the chanted ritual of exorcism, combined with all those remaining on our planet, is near indescribable. All differentiation evaporated, or did it integrate? The intensity was so enormous I could not think.

Would I implode or explode? How can I describe to you this extraordinary state holding no direction, space or time, and beyond the range of human emotion? The Cysts were shattered in their ships. With eyes bursting and their skulls splitting, they fell screeching with hands over their faces and ears, snake tongues lashing out, their spines arching into spasms of agony until in their last efforts of coordination they turned their ships in flight back to where they belonged with the words of exorcism burning their brains. I mused and pondered if it might have been better had we been able to subdue the enemy without fighting. That surely would have been the epitome of skill!

(\*) In Galactic symbolism of flames supported in a seven-branched golden candlestick is an alchemical metaphor for Man having perfected his seven principles. The Voice of many waters alludes to the many seas of Space permeated by the Word of Consciousness. The seven stars of Ursa Major, combined with the Pleiades, were astronomical time markers for your planet's early epochs in the formation of your race recorded in the Vedas. The stars were portals of power for great Cosmic Beings (named Richis by the Indians), some of whom were said to have in long gone ages incarnated as men. Others made humans the vehicles of their reflection through inspiration. They were the archetype within the confines of their own creation. They were gods among men, but not gods amongst gods. Among them are Galactics and Anunnaki who have mingled with you Earthlings throughout your evolution.

---

*It is for you to take your pick of how you view redemption or ascension, concerning all species of human and humanoid creations. Is there a meaning to life, or has it only the meaning we give to it?*

*In the primeval depths of our consciousness lie the seeds of forgetfulness.*

*Keresch axiom.*

## CHAPTER 16. CELEBRATIONS AND REMEMBRANCE

Back on our planet, on exceptional occasions such as our accomplishment with the Cysts, we bring down the two fire crystals, blue-white, and red-purple from our main cave. Placed in the middle of our ceremonial valley they tower like twin dolmens emanating their power. They keep equilibrium between the yin and the yang in the energy of our planet.

Our priestly caste gathered in full attire of deep purple cloaks lined with gold, flowing over long, loose trousers caught at the ankles and belted shirts in a white weave that glowed with its own life. In a slow movement, five abreast, they formed a figure of eight around the crystals, each carrying a manifested cool flame nestled in their cupped hands. Encircling them stood a multitude of our women warriors and many older women, as well as teachers who were not necessarily called to fight.

They sang in a chorus of changing harmonics, the sound of the voices in perfect harmony pulsed gently, rising and falling in volume. Beyond them swung five great circles of men, each with outstretched arms resting on each other's shoulders. They stamped out intricate rhythms, sometimes leaping or bending with each movement, imitating the undulating body of a cosmic serpent. A cluster of bells attached to each ankle could have been the song of water and wind moving in the air, or even a brilliant fire crackling through autumn's dried twigs.

Every Keresch male knew the intricacies of this dance, learnt from the time he entered our world. It was a ritual, and in ritual we express the multiple vibrations of our planet, placing ourselves as transformers of energies. It was during this festival, culminating in the great ring dance, that I caught sight of Yoneck again. He had remained on our planet to maintain our protective devices during the war. Upholding his custom from the time of our childhood friendship, he was the first to greet and embrace me on my return. Yoneck, my Commander and me had reincarnated together. I knew they remembered our past, but I haplessly, even from an early age, had unsuccessfully sought the answers to my forgetfulness. How had I escaped in Atlantis? Why had Ayesha deserted me?

The priests smiled at such questions. They nodded sympathetically then shook their heads. I had to do my own work in recall. I could search the Aetheric archives or regress under dangerous mind-altering techniques. Hypnotism, in your sense, was not an option for the way our lobes interact. For all the possibilities at my disposal I still feared any process of recall. In the depths of my being, beyond reach, I felt the Anunnaki during my capture had mangled part of my being to pulp in a psychic violation that could span many incarnations. I avoided recall by chaining myself to the fear of fear and hid behind patience, cultivating a passive hope for remembrance.

To overcome this form of a curse I knew it rested on some person, some object, smell, touch, sound, or taste that would unlock the bars of my prison. I had to wait and be vigilant. One of my teachers had once said:

"You must learn to taste through your eyes, smell with your ears, hear with your nose, and see through your fingers. Become what you were before your senses were separated. The higher your senses, the greater will be your connections with your BA." Bizarre it is when the hoped- for situation arrives unexpectedly without an obvious association with the desired result. In my case, the recall of that devastating event in a previous life wiped from conscious memory, came with the sight of Yoneck swinging past me in the whirling ring dance of our victory celebrations.

Our eyes met in laughter. A trapdoor opened and I fell into memory.

It is the year when the autumn harvest in the north island of Atlantis is profusely represented in a mountain of various grains stacked in tiered sheathes at the gate of our main amphitheatre. The local Atlanteans have incorporated their theatrical arts with ours in a cross-cultural spectacle. Encouraged by the Anunnaki lords, regarded by most as visiting gods from a star world with whom we are in league, the festival opens with a roar of anticipation greeting the thick processions. The parading crowds are barbaric in ornament and inventive dress. They march to the pounding of deep drums and horns, their ranks interspersed with wild, swirling fire-eaters.

Their voices raised in song bring smiles of appreciation to all levels of society, from the overlords to those they have trained in service to work in the hierarchy of that epoch. Yoneck dances with our people in waves of advancing and retreating warriors, imitating our classic strategy in battle. He sings a paean accompanied by Atlantean harps, enormous instruments each plucked by seven players. I see myself being drawn to him in a sweet agony of heart.

Need I continue with the obvious story of our later taking an oath of allegiance? In my newfound excitement, I lose all consideration for my Commander. His presence, banished from my mind, withers into an obscurity. I watch myself in horror, appalled by my thoughtless conduct. It is usual when a Keresch takes on a second allegiance, he or she feels no need to abandon the previous liaison. To the contrary, I become confined and blinkered when joining Yoneck in ecstasy common to our kind. Of course Ayesha must have instantly known this and felt my unnecessary disregard for his relationship with me. Although our protocol stresses how to avoid inept ways of conduct in emotionally sensitive situations, too obviously I had not held faith, whereas Yoneck had communicated to Ayesha our happiness, as well as his sadness in my lack of consideration.

Why had I deserted him?

I have already disclosed how shortly after my allegiance with Yoneck I saw two Anunnaki disappear on the hill alongside our Birthing Rotunda. Following them, I descended like Eurydice into the underworld, into horror, into oblivion. It took this incarnation to finally awaken recollections of what had happened and what I had done to Ayesha. Now, on catching Yoneck's eye at the time of the ring dance of our victory celebrations, my sight, the sense most acutely connected to my reactions in the Anunnaki underground laboratory, sucked me back to my previous life in Atlantis, to relationships, to the Anunnaki, and proceeded to trigger the missing component of my sojourn in Hades.

I see myself floating in a transparent coffin. I see a figure in grey approach; it tilts the lid and gently eases me out. I crumple on the floor, naked. The figure takes off the grey covering revealing a second coat underneath. On being clothed in the first coat I watch myself opening my eyes. I enter into the image of myself to look at the figure helping me to half-crawl, half-walk across the floor. She is Manisa, the mother of the twins. I try to speak with no success.

Manisa shakes her head, urging me on towards a narrow cage suspended in a tube. "They promised me," she whispers, "that I could see my babies if I worked for them, kept silent, kidnapped? newborns when needed, otherwise I would be turned into a sub-human mindless thing."

I understand, unable to reply other than grunt. Manisa drags me into the cage and lies on top of me on our ascent into a storage room for vats of plasma derived from the chemicals of your Earth.

I can stand for a few moments before falling to the ground. Manisa gives me phials of liquid to swallow, pulls what resembles a counterweight lever to a door, and pushes me out saying, "Go straight. It leads up to the desert. There is a moon. Walk away from your shadow and in a while you will come to a village. I hope they will help."

I lie dazed. When I turn to look back at the door that I knew had closed behind me, there is nothing, only a small hill. The frequencies have been changed. I stagger and crawl my way by moonlight in an arduous journey with little memory of anything or anyone, other than my arrival at the sea, already told, and the struggle to coordinate a message to my home planet.

---

Every image had come and gone in a flash. From finding the past in the present, I was freed to make my own amends to those I loved, including the woman once called Manisa (who would reincarnate with me in Egypt). With the help of Yoneck she had escaped, and I knew our meeting was a future certainty, hopefully with her twins.

Fully returned to the present, I looked up at my Commander standing next to me in the celebrations. He smiled without words. Yoneck laughed when he caught my eye from the leaping, undulating ring of warriors dancing to the dense beat of our music. He and Ayesha, in their unhindered recall of events from our last incarnations together, had never tried in any way to remind me of my behaviour. They had waited for time itself to turn the key in the door of my heart, the seat of my *BA* that held the power to overcome the Anunnaki curse. How gratifying it was that I had found release in our mass thanksgiving for work well done in the chaining of the Cysts. In a personal exorcism I was cleansed from the presence of the dark Anunnaki.

A few days later we gathered with friends, Bannerman and Ayesha's colleagues, three men and two women, in Ayesha's home on the sides of the Crystal Mountains. I sensed it would be an important occasion for me.

"You have proved that your constitution can withstand the pressures on every level found on planet Earth," said my Commander, after a memorable meal. "Mine cannot." He continued, "My work remains in this density with an outsider's view. I will be waiting, watching, and I trust never wanting in my work with a group consciousness for what has to be achieved." He paused, then continued, "The decision is yours. You can reject or take this mission I am about to offer. It is in preparation for extraordinary changes on Earth in a far future."

I freely chose my path in agreement with Ayesha's proposal. It led me into a long series of incarnations in the flesh of your kind, enriched with a unique genetic code that will bloom fully in time to come. In a short, traditional ceremony held in our main hall of the Crystal Mountains, so intrinsic to our culture and power, the priests anointed me by scattering over my head magnetized dust from a pulverized fire crystal. They fluttered down in that wondrous cave as my Commander called out my emblematic name.

His voice hit the rocks in intervals, echoing against the vaulted ceiling, and I felt safety in my name, Ni Tekad the Survivor, one who has withstood the psychic and physical violence of the Anunnaki, one who is ready to continue the work begun with Earthlings in Atlantis.

This was my freely accepted identification I could change any time. It was not my identity.

Had I decided to access the Aetheric records, had I concentrated and brought my awareness to focus on my past nightmare, had I with full desire from heart and head decided to remember, doubtless my lack of recall would have been retrieved to the benefit of strengthening the crystalline core of my incarnated being. Instead, I had cheated myself, and fear above all emotions had delayed my progress.

---

*Who is more foolish, the child afraid of the dark Or the man afraid of the light?*

*Maurice Freehill 1899-1939*

*Patience, like a memory, is a balance swung across the heart,*
*the scales of contemplation where each act of mind is weighed before ascension.*
*So must I fly and swing and wing throughout the flux of life*
*until in ancient days I sing with manifold experience.*

*Keresch ballad of Remembrance.*

*There exists only the present... a Now*
*Which always and without end is itself new.*
*There is no yesterday nor any tomorrow, but only*
*Now, as it was a thousand years ago and as it*
*Will be a thousand years hence.*

*Meister Eckhart 1260-1327*

## CHAPTER 17. THE PRESENT

On Earth, sanctified in the West with sanitation and the homogenization of being programmed throughfear, too many of you are stripped of your soul and dismembered from your spirit. At times in this bareness I have ached with the memory of music from my homeland with its echo smothered in distance, but I must not fall into lugubrious lament.

Beyond this matter, in my present sojourn in this world under the protective eye of my Commander, half my time has been devoted to remembering, adjusting karmic bonds, and meeting anew certain people while I wandered the wilds of Earth.

One burnished autumn, the pattern of my life brought me into the presence of an art dealer in America, a thin, fragile man, unremarkable before I looked into his transparent eyes.

"You are not as tall as you once were," he remarked on our meeting, and in confirming my instant recognition, we brought forth the past together. This pale-eyed man, he, the most High Priest, Guardian and Ancient One, verified everything I had remembered from our past affiliations.

"It is difficult enough to impart sacred information," he continued with his slightly crooked smile, "and even more challenging to explain the progression, the unfolding of the principles of Man until he returns to where he never left."

"We are reflections of our Immortal Spirit," I answered. "Yet," he continued, " how magnificent to imagine that when the BA unites with its original other half in the higher realms, it is known as *AKHU.*

Then when finally drawn up into Origin, the Spark of Life together with all the principles of previous manifestation are replaced by the Flame, also known as *SEKHEM*, the Immortal Spirit in Origin. It is no less than man transfigured." He expanded this subject by reminding me of the Egyptian text from the tomb of Pepe II in the old kingdom. It writes:

> *I am purified of all imperfections, what is it? I ascend like the golden hawk of Horus, what is it? I come by the immortals without dying, what is it? I come before my father's throne, and what are these attributes that you acquire as you ascend?*

One meaning is a reference to taking monoatomic gold, other metal powders, or organic substances, opening your perceptions to higher frequencies. The repeated question can also be asking for the names, and thus the definition and understanding of the refined attributes belonging to the higher psychic principles with their subtle frequencies received when you are in contact with the BA, your golden Horus hawk, that, in the higher manifestations of matter, unites with its original partner before being drawn up into Origin. On the whole, the texts carry the message of the alchemist: awareness establishes its corresponding reality. Enlarge consciousness and you transmute yourself and your environment into a higher order.

"And what have you learnt in this life?" he asked, smiling gently.

"That Osiris, in one aspect, is just a reminder of what we have forgotten. I am my own judge. My *Higher Mind*, my Osiris/BA, adjudicates my progression back into *Flame*." I wondered if there were any correspondence between his and my childlike vision of glory, in which Light came with Fire, the mysterious and mystic bipolar element that illuminates all Heavens and most Hells of earthly beliefs.

Grounded in happiness and peace, I left only to hear of his death a few months later. It left me sad for not having been more grateful at our meeting. He had, as we like to say, gone home. I thought that we would have had more time together for him to continue his explanations and memories spiced with his reminiscence of the secret work he and colleagues had accomplished in this world. They rightly will never be known. In this life he was a hidden master of metaphysics, having worked with others like himself. He told me that this time round he had lived successively for over 250 years, and carried unbroken recall in each incarnation.

Only months later I suddenly understood the enormous significance of his last words before we parted. I had spoken of the soul at death being weighed for ascension against the weight of a feather on the scales of justice. "Live rightly, live well, and your heart will be as light as a feather. Be happy!" he had called raising his right hand in a subdued wave. At the time the simplicity of his last two hackneyed words flew over my head until I remembered that a happy heart broadcasts energy fed by the hormones released in this state. They raise your vibrations, as already explained in the chapter on our birth chambers.

Another such remarkable person met in my wanderings was a Tibetan monk I had the privilege to meet for one short, cold morning. Escape from his homeland took him to Bhutan, and there, after seven years in a cave, for all his knowledge he became no important abbot, but taught from a little stone hut. Taking my head in his hands he placed the top of his forehead to mine. In that gesture he gave the blessings of an unknown Avatar to all beings in his presence. Behind his shy smile I sensed a person who, in the safety of anonymity, in transmuting immense suffering in the perdition of this world, had found immeasurable compassion beyond normal comprehension. He had dispersed the pain of a multitude of humans by digesting it through himself.
It was the litmus of what he was: an anchor of Light. No longer on Earth, he, the Beloved, remains in contact with the people who love him.

Metaphysics, from the verbosity of the 19th century, is currently being clarified with a new, at times pseudo-scientific, vocabulary which includes a multitude of words: from quantum (are ideas meant to jump 'discreetly' like atomic particles from one condition to another? to interdimensional, multidimensional, hyperspace, vibration, matrix, and any amount of electrical terms.

Then there is the terminology of harmonics and resonance, progressing to entwined frequencies, reflection spaces, densities, genetic helix, junk genes, holograms, fractals, genome, alternative realities, parallel universes, vortices, zero point energy, portals, timelines, string theory, scalar energy, HAARP, morphic resonance and many other things permitting God, gods, angels, the devil, to congeal into a long verbal equation of information, omitting, in this tale, the doctrine of soul contracts and their karma conjunct with ascension and redemption. It is easier to follow if one accepts that all matter is vibration. The power of thought affects everything we do, be it an experiment in particle physics or our attitude to each other. What would you say were you to know that CERN, outwardly a particle accelerator, is an infernal time machine built to numb your mind and dreams?

Your studies in epigenetics are forging ahead in understanding the interaction between genes and your actions and reactions in life. In over-simplistic terms, genes find their expression in behaviour, and behaviour, born from thoughts and emotion, loops back to affects change in the genetic structure. Mind is Consciousness in a relationship between itself and manifestations brought into being on a foundation of mathematical structures and frequencies. They form three-dimensional, intermingling Platonic and Archimedean shapes, projected from the Aether (the higher aspect of Ether) into your dimension. Each manifestation takes form on geometric structures containing their own organising intelligence. Some ancient signs and symbols still exist that hold this form of intelligence within their shapes and with which you can communicate.

We have observed Earthlings and helped give out information with other Galactics over the cycles of time. We have observed you pass through contempt for your flesh, without ever doubting the existence of another reality waiting, as either Heaven or Hell for your soul when separated by death from the body. You have tried to reach spirit by denying the flesh. At present, immersed in materialism, your science ploughs through matter as if it were a body hidden by the dance of the seven veils which once discarded will expose the existence of Spirit. It really will!

We have seen your capacity to survive and keep your sense of humor, a trait I am proud to say we helped insert in your being. Although denied the advantages of our particular constitution, many of you belong to the family of Galactic man, but it still leaves a fair quantity of your brilliant minds limited to the immediate material reality, refusing to admit the validity of psychic phenomena until it is somehow reduced to the codes of your recent science, awash with new theories of matter and its *origin*.

I have spent much of the present existence giving back lost information to people and recording in words and images the rites of vanishing tribes. You are losing your sense of ritual and celebration, each a form of commitment to an event or an idea, raising it from the mundane to a time worthy of remembrance.

The process of ritual performed with intention and attention releases electromagnetic currents and neurological reactions that mark the subconscious… unless thoughtless repetition reduces the routine to mumbo-jumbo.

The rituals of the tribal peoples in remote jungles, those in your towered cities, or ours in our valley of the crystal caves, if differing in content, are the same in the basic process. Whether the rituals are for Light or for Darkness, they use the same source of power either to harm, help, enslave (as did the Anunnaki), or liberate.

In my travels near forty years ago, I attended the ceremonies of the richest temple in India. They were extraordinarily similar to those I remembered so vividly in Egypt. Dressed as a Hindu, a lone European at that time, I passed with other pilgrims through a low, dark tunnel, into the glow of a stifling womb-shaped room with flames casting shimmering light on a nine-foot high black basalt stature of the Lord Vishnu. At his feet stood numerous gold statues of consorts and sacred utensils. His arms and legs were sheathed in diamonds. A five-inch emerald hung flashing from a thick, a 30 kg gold chain on his chest. Across his face lay a narrow camphor band hiding one eye, closed in compassion, while the other left open, assessed those who came before him with thanks or to ask for favours. Adorning his head rose a beehive crown in a mass of small diamonds and precious gems.

One of the arrogant Brahmin priests, a young medical student at Harvard, said that evening in a matter of fact voice, "When I anoint the Lord with perfumed oil, I can feel the movement of breath beneath the stone."

Standing before this magnetic figure I made a wish. It was granted. Fifteen years later, although the price of joy and sadness had proved high, in retrospect I understood its purpose, and how periods of stress had been the goad pushing me onto my final path.

On another day I watched a small, richly dressed and jewel-laden replica of Lord Vishnu in an enormous over-decorated carriage encrusted with priests, being pulled by hundreds of men through the town. It rolled its way to a flower-covered swing before the temple. My river of memory ran back to the similar temple ceremonies in Egypt and the morning rites in the House of Ptah.

On the island of Bali, further Egyptian recollections of my death and rebirth resurged when a certain high priest invited me to the inauguration of his son after the comparable initiation of leaving his body in a cataleptic state for over 24 hours. On his return to this world, photographs were allowed in the course of the celebrations. One photo, and one only, showed the new high priest coming from prayers in the family temple with his forehead marked by a fiery orange and red circle. It proved to be no trick of light on the lens, or a squashed marigold pressed in blessing on his forehead. It was a psychic occurrence of a blazing chakra, the presence of a spirit being, and a blessing from his gods. Highly sacred, the enlarged photo, covered by a white cloth to shield it from the masses with their vampire gaze, was hung in the meeting pavilion of his home.

Another time on a sultry night at full moon in a graveyard with dogs howling, I sat next to a Balinese shaman who had promised to manifest Fire in his hand. After a time of incantations, a large, elongated flame appeared, its tip just touching his palm. When he placed its white, electromagnetic-cold, and steady light to rest in the palm of my hand I was so entranced that I forgot to ask an accompanying friend to take a photo, an untoward request since the Balinese surrounding me clung together in terror. The shaman forthwith commanded me to swallow the flame, supposedly to heal my damaged lung. I did. It was no more than putting air into my mouth.

Half an hour later, with an unexpectedly menacing look, he said he would remove the flame from my stomach or I might become extremely ill because this white light becomes a malignant intelligence, an entity that continues to live within you, feeding and growing on your vitality. Once home, my Balinese friends told me why they had been very worried during the course of events in the graveyard. I had crossed the threshold of safety. This shaman used the black arts to manifest objects or to cure. Others used white magic. According to the Balinese both options work, and all shamans have to know the two sides of power before choosing which aspect to use. Some who walked the dark path always vowing they would change later, a purpose seldom completed. Shamans, very selective in accepting pupils, are generally egotistic and individualistic. Each owns a lineage of ancestral information passed on verbally or in sacred writings used in their home locality.

Before knowing how both the Dark and the Light can cure I was confused in observing over time the methods of one infamous healer. He cured menstrual and other female disorders, also terrifyingly enlarged scrotums, by placing his mouth over the genitals and sucking. He stated that the spirit of a leech god inhabited him. When an American woman and her ailing daughter arrived, the daughter pulled up her skirt. The Shaman went to work. The mother shrieked and fainted. Called over to observe, I watched him suck and then pass the ends of his long hair over the girl's pubic regions. I noticed the ends were covered in small, shining drops of moisture. He asked me to bend and smell, and there came the scent of fresh flowers and seawater. Later, the girl was reported in fine health, but within eight years the Shaman, paralysed, died in an uncomfortable death, and other patients found that the payments were Faustian.

The manipulation of subtle energy I first witnessed while crouching down during an immensely powerful trance ritual. One of the men wearing an empowered demonic mask raced in silence past me, his feet at least five inches off the ground.

Another village shaman I was acquainted with sat happily on the fence, receiving high payment for efficient curses and equally high fees for protecting babies from earth demons during the ceremony of putting their feet on the ground for the first time when they come into contact with the lower earth spirits. In Bali, noted for its dark magicians, harming or killing a person is of no consequence to them. It is no more than a power game with the practitioners of the black arts often ending up struck down with painful and debilitating illness.

Few Balinese condemn black magic believing retribution is due, if not in this life, then surely the next. I have observed the power used in shape-shifting during possession, its energy so different from that witnessed in other equally unusual acts of calling a departed spirit to return to a cataleptic body after an accident, and after the doctors had given up hope.

One of the island's most revered high priests was called upon after a large landslide. Five bodies lay smothered by the deep mud. The priest was asked to locate them. He took his time sitting in meditation with lowered eyes.

"What's the matter?" asked one of the villagers.

"Be patient!" he answered. "It's very dark in here." To their sad delight, he located the bodies exactly, and with much labour the dead were retrieved for all the mandatory death rituals of such vital importance to the Balinese Hindus. As they say on this Prospero's isle of deities and demons:

*The brighter the Light, the darker the Shadow.*

Although many celebrations for the holy are today diminished and crushed by materialism, I found in tribal societies an instinct, however diluted, that keep them in tenuous communication with the invisible powers shaping and affecting this world. One year in France there came a man to our village. Stocky, still strong but aging, he was a retired priest walking around in dusty black and unpolished shoes. On hearing that he was the late exorcist attached to the Cathedral of Notre Dame in Paris, I invited him for tea. After polite chit-chat I asked how the Devil chooses those he possesses. Surely being very clever, he would enter the body and mind of those with the highest intelligence. His answer was informative. "The Devil," he replied, "could only enter someone with an inherently flawed psyche." He went on to tell that after spending 30 years in Sri Lanka combatting all manner of local magic, he had dealt with but four satanic possessions in his life.

One was little more than a child, and when inhabited by a devil had bent a 20 cm long iron crucifix. All other cases of supposed possession in Sri Lanka or France, he had sent packing to a doctor or psychiatrist.

On seeing him leave his heavy shoulders gave the impression of still holding great power. Had I been a devil I would not have enjoyed meeting him under any circumstance. Other spirit contacts I frequently observed in tribal societies were called from the realms of Nature to inhabit a medium through ritual trance. Dying cultures and their beliefs have been condemned as perpetuating ignorant superstitions to sedate fear. Partly correct, it ignores those who have used mind-altering substances, that, when taken responsibly, lead to extraordinary places inhabited by beings of another genre in another realm alongside of earth.

Personal mystic experience, unless shared in exceptional cases, cannot be transferred to another person's reality. It has to be lived through and integrated into an individual's own comprehension. Tribal people, termed primitive, accept other realities, high or low, and preserve an open heart with reverence for an order beyond the material, an emotion you have to find again and adapt to your present era.

To lose touch with the power of the unseen is to lose a lot. People from the third world with few intellectual barriers retain an inherent ability to tune into other realities usually smothered by disbelief, although not necessarily lost to the western person educated to be sceptical about anything not proven by science.

Some neurologists theorize on the workings of the mind without experiencing alternative states. They give mathematical and intellectual hypotheses for neurologically recorded 'modes of observation' in the effort to correlate into their systems what they think are subjective hallucinations beyond conventional reality.

If you reach into the fabled states of shamans, as the scientist/philosopher Alfred NorthWhitehead says, "What you call substance is shadow and shadow, the substance." Shamans are manipulators, masters in the power of thought projection, even if few of them have the gift of love in your personal sense. Others will call their art a psychic control used to influence the masses. True enough there are witches, warlocks of the Left Hand path, but, on the positive side, acceptance of multiple realities leads humanity out from its confined existence.

166

The Anunnaki conditioned so many of you to worship them as self-proclaimed gods of your material creation. The imprint of this inbuilt propensity for devotion is an ambiguous double-edged sword. Cut the Gordian knot of subservience while preserving reverence for higher things understood by expanding your heart. Appreciate not the controllers but beauty itself, the first step to awareness and wonder should you look up to a star encrusted sky or watch the molten orb of a rising sun. I have spoken so often about polarity, the two sides of a single coin, and if better known, the presence of the Anunnaki will reveal that among them were people of fair intent whose efforts in genetic adaption benefited your evolution, contrary to the aim of others working for domination, not progress.

We have placed nodes in your genome that, like secret switches, will thrust you forward when activated on your own volition at this time of your planet's mutating electromagnetic activity brought about in its passage into new areas, new conditions, and new frequencies on the immense rim of your rotating galaxy in its course through space.

It is time again to recollect and dream.

I pass into rivers of remembrance and lift my eyes to the Milky Way with its flow symbolically mirrored in the earthly counterpart of the sacred Nile, carrying all memories of Egypt from the time those you call gods came down to Earth. I leap from the past to the present and stand again on the banks of the river Ganga, descending from the Himalayan snows and monsoon rains in such terrifying abundance that the waters could have fallen from Heaven itself.

Their fall, softened in the net of Shiva's hair, then flowed on across the heat and dust of the Indian plains: all homage to Mother Ganga! Mystics tell that:

> Ions ago the Ganges fell from Mars accompanied by souls leaving that planet to reincarnate on earth. They passed from unseen dimension of a hihger frequency in a process beyond our publicly eccepted physic, and the great river having decended from its origin to its Himalayan source, carries properties not of this world.

The liquid crystal atomic structure of Ganga water is verifiably different, even in the face of it being one of the foremost-polluted rivers on your planet. Ganga, like her sister Nile, is a River from Heaven. She represents her mythic celestial counterpart, and for the Hindus the river carries the power of the Lord Shiva, the Redeemer of all living creatures. Sanskrit texts record him coming to his chosen site of Benares, also known as Karshi and Varenesi, on the banks of this most sacred waterway.

Here he returns in person to whisper wisdom in the ear of those waiting to die. Even today to die in Karshi, the Hindus believe, is to be liberated, freed from illusion, to return to the source of Spirit, that which one is:

*Tat tvam asi.*

Thus were the cosmic teachings of the mighty Shiva passed on in an oral tradition from the time of the Sky Peoples' intervention in the affairs of Earth. For the Hindus their ancient teachings are eternal, coming from cyclically revealed wisdom.

So many of your great rivers, synonymous with myth and unseen powers retold by the Ancient Ones in tales of layered meaning, are still revered as holding living deities. The mystic properties of your world's Fire, Air, Earth, and Water were used to release the soul from the body, and through unrecorded years in the oral tradition of the Vedas, Mother Ganga carried the ashes of the cremated to the sea.

Where Karshi now stands, for eons until a few hundred years ago, there grew thick forests with groves in which India's first tribes worshipped the spirits of Nature. They were seen clearly with an inner eye, not yet clouded as Earthlings became more condensed and attached to matter. In those distant days we came to teach dance, rhythm, and the significance of different keys in music. It was a joyful experience, successful in balancing the nascent inner light of those gentle people, already so sensitive to colour. We taught them ritual to steady their concentration, perhaps a little too successfully, because as a means to an end, it became the end itself, declining into mechanical repetition more than being a lens to consciously focus energy into the heart chakra.

The arrival of interdimensional visitors coming down as gods was conveniently appropriate for the local people. They imitated local spirits of Nature, or taking on the personae of kings, perpetuated their line, and ruled with divine authority passed down in so many of your cultures. From worshipping Nature in nature, temples holding fire on their altars housed crude idols of elemental spirits and later those of their 'heavenly rulers.'

And Shiva, that immense cosmic intelligence so often recalled as being present at the beginning of creation, came again into India in the form of a Galactic Master circa 140,000 years ago. This happened at the same time as a full scale Anunnaki intervention with other Aliens interested in your species. Similar to the Babylonian myths, they too produced monstrous animal forms. Since other enlightened Galactics opposed these agendas, the complex interrelationships between men of Earth and their overlords evolved into conflicting groups, even among the Anunnaki themselves. The great gods of India, if not Nature Spirits beheld with the inner eye, were interdimensional men and women visiting, or later incarnating, in genetically mixed bodies. The Anunnaki promptly usurped the name and presence of Shiva, the very name carrying power in its sound and letters. As the texts say, he travels from the heights of the Himalayas with his wife Parvati, he becomes master of the river land with his seat in Karshi. He commands all other deities. He absorbs all local beliefs in a diguised form of mastership.

He modifies genetics and has his offspring plus a rout of imposters uphold his authority. In part, India's ancient texts hold exhaustingly rambling accounts of the interaction between Celestials, the Underworld of demons and Earthling tribes, with the latter lengthily exhorting their godly (usually Annunaki) pedigrees of superior genealogy. All the while, to keep the balance between warring factions, the Guardians, the Wise Ones, act as neutral observers who watch the Anunnaki usurp Lord Shiva's name. They permit the usurper to forward his plans. Pretending to agree, in their ruse they know that the seed of the Anunnaki transmitted and transmuted in their genetic meddling, will eventually find liberation through Earthlings. You will absorb and transmute the genetic cross, the mythic cross reaching from the heights to the depths, and in your progress you will take your progenitors (those who choose) with you.

The origin of the Vedas profoundly associated with the sound of AUM, the eternal vibration of creativity and dissolution, was first brought to man on your planet in the cosmic cycle the Hindus call the Treta Yuga, the era when they say that great divinities descended on Earth. They lived for thousands of years... or their direct reincarnations did, and like shards from a shattered mirror they reincarnated again and again to continue their work. The Treta Yuga illuminated by three Avatars, each an incarnation of Vishnu (another great cosmic architect associated with Shiva), lasted according to the Hindus for 1,296,000 years before the next cycle, the Dvarpa Yuga ran for 864,000 years, followed by the present Kali Yuga starting about 3,000 years ago, and said to continue for over 60,000 years.

These great Galactic beings, with helpers described in the Vedas, revealed knowledge progressively given out in relation to your evolution. When the successive teachers themselves became corrupted and lost their lustre from intermingling with Earthlings, their offspring nonetheless were deemed as demigods, some from Light, others from the lower states of vibration.

We had our preferred groups supported over many incarnations. With other Galactics we came again in number to teach archery, medicine, music, dance, and military science.

Each subject was a part of the oral and then recorded Vedic tradition in the time of the Dvarpa Yuga. This was before the change into the present Kali Yuga with humanity declining in, as is said, age, virtue, and understanding. In the violent conflicts of the Mahabharata (recorded around 1,500 BC after ages of precise oral transmission, its method still known todayspace-age technology with flying machines and high cities in the air that was reported in terms understood at that time. Other Vedic texts include extraordinary mathematical and coded information together with moral injunctions and the philosophy of existence still relevant when examined by your advanced thinkers. And the seemingly endless near repetitive hymns of praise hold word combinations, mantras, letters with number and sound that, if read in one direction, give coded data, and, if read in the opposite direction or in a changing sequence, reveal other meanings not as yet fully deciphered. Many of the complicated stories, not unlike the Greek Pantheon, are filled with bad behaviour, blood feuds, and violence.

Their themes often give the impression that the original wisdom derived from another reality has grown inward into complication, having lost its original power encased in symbols. The Sanskrit language, said to have come from a heavenly origin like its counterpart, Egyptian hieroglyphs, claims to keep eternal verity by never altering the sound and meaning of words regardless of all change in your world. Today this theory can be sadly diminished through forgetfulness.

In this life, when on the steep stone steps of Benares, I gave praise to the rising sun, shedding a misty glamour on the rot and filth lying against her banks. I took a boat into the middle of the great, grey-green, greasy Ganga and stayed there, enveloped in a strange peace exuding from an ineffable atmosphere of devotion. In the early sunlight the shabby yet impressive buildings glowed in an ethereal atmosphere.

Light flashed off brass pots and the sound of a flute rested on the air as I watched people wash in the slime, sewage, and ash of cremated bodies, never doubting the sanctity of the river, even if their faith does not always shield them from disease. Water drawn from a metre below the surface is surprisingly clear. Every evening, priests chanted, circling pyramids of fire in triangular candlesticks. Photographs later revealed (their authenticity hotly disputed by your scientists) a gathering of transparent spirit orbs suspended in the air around us. Heavy brass bells toiled, conches boomed, and the devout sent sweet flowers and candles to float away with prayers on black water under moonlight. This is the point where the natural and spiritual worlds meet. Tirtha, the word for blessed water, also means the ford, a place of crossing. Benares is the place where souls pass from one life to another. Here myth, mystery, and geography morph into a strange, lightly veiled phenomena that hovers just above the ground.

Not in hearsay but in truth, in Shiva's golden temple on certain ceremonies giving homage to his sacred stone Lingam, priests of a most ancient order recite mantras in an unknown tongue, said to have been repeated for over 10,000 years.

I saw in those teeming crowds of poverty something barely discernable: the glimmer of potential Man with a possibility of a future flame from oil in an unlit lamp not yet sullied by materialism.

From the essence of filth rose an enduring faith, given spiritual potency with constantly renewed rituals. Mechanical or not, prayer repeated every day and night over untold centuries, has sustained an energy beyond the corruption of men. Faith springs from sacred history rooted in myth: its manifold interpretations portray the human condition. On the burning ghats of Benares apparently nothing holds ghosts in the air. With the smoke from charred bones they depart content in release from this life.

According to their belief, by grace from Shiva uttering in the ear of the dying, the mantra AUM, the verbal symbol of the supreme reality, souls rise into bliss beyond reincarnation. Their essence returns to the essence from where it came. Tat tvam asi, 'That art thou.'

Since religion is the history of faith, the passive Hindu masses wait for Shiva's AUM to lift their souls to heaven. In contrast, a Westerner, in his own words, proclaims his sovereign identity with a poem independent of any conventional ritual.

*Formlessness - dear friends, is the hallmark of my*
*enterprise I am the voice of reason, I am the tracer of events*
*My expression is without opinion, my recitation*
*without regard My narration is fuelled by the*
*unfolding story*
*I am without projection as I am without reflection*
*I am founded in neither logic nor lore*
*I am the sole principle which is without effect*
*I am the principle which governs all principles*
*Mine alone is the movement which carries no consequence*
*What I speak of is what stirs*
*As that which stirs - would be spoken of*
*Nothing is beholden to me and all is beheld by me*
*If I am spoken of - it is as the telling foretold*

*I proffer questions to questions and reflect answers to answers*
*I am the mirror that mirrors the mirror*
*I am not by degrees and mine is the locus without relativity*
*I am neither instrument nor vehicle*
*conduit nor vessel*
*I am without purpose as I am without pledge*
*I am the witness without witness*
*I am that I am*

What if you saw those crowds, their predicament, their state of mind and body as little more than expendable and disposable cannon fodder or slave labour? What if you look at this world as a glass half full, ready to be filled, or half empty, awaiting emptiness? Choose! And that is the reality in which you will live.

Simple as this may sound, there will be times when you wish to change your outlook due to circumstance, for at the best of times an attitude in dealing with the human condition is not necessarily a constant. Impressive and unexpectedly beautiful in its contrasts, Benares, perhaps the oldest continuously inhabited city in your world, is where Shiva and the Buddha taught, not forgetting that there have been many Shivas and many Buddhas.

However, time has come for a different interpretation of dogma. More than bodies have to be cleansed in fire. Now in a reversed process, in attention to the matter of flesh so long despised in your search for spirit, hopefully some of your scientists will discover the soul's existence through the physics of vibration. In linking soul to matter, I return to the Agari of Benares.

Not always beggars, some are successful businessmen who have renounced this world. Terrible indeed are their practices of embracing the filth of existence. Covered in ashes, they decapitate a corpse to use its head as a bowl for collecting food. They sleep on graves, cook over the embers of cremation, and on occasions devour the flesh of the dead.

Call them the dark left hand of Shiva, those who in loathing nothing in life or death transcend dualism to be liberated from all worlds of illusion. Only they can affirm their hopes. Although I do not wish to belittle the essence of reverence found in this ancient city of many Ghats, the Hindus themselves, most likely with tongue in cheek, speak of their gods being worried that if too many humans find liberation here without fulfilling their karma, heaven will become overcrowded; even worse there will not be enough human emotion needed for their deities' survival! Surely this is a snide reminder of the lock and key the Anunnaki created in keeping planet Earth as their domain.

Reverence is essential in understanding the wonder of creation. Worship in subservience embedded in control is another matter.

From the burning Ghats of Benares I pass in mind through the portals of the underworld into the light of fires and smoke in the weeping places of battlefields. I come to retrieve my dead, mourn them, and burn their bodies on great pyres of honour to their courage and respect to their ancestors.

They are all metaphors for the pain, fear, and violence of Earth, including memories of false myths and dreams that must die as they hold the resonance of failure. I move and am contacted by a wraith of a man.

He leads me to the vault of my own dead laid on a tilted slab. I see decaying flesh and bone. In my mind's eye I transform them back into the great golden horde, the giants of old who first came to Earth and were mutilated. I weep. Gigantic white oxen transport them out on a groaning wagon with each body now encased in an open barred coffin studded with gems. I stand aside as the procession moves into mists. And in that crack between the dimensional, the liminal, and the imagined, in that magic space and place, I offer up the bodies on a pyre to be consumed in a flash of Fire and Air.

They are the corpses of multitudes of reincarnations, saluted, and their essence given back to the essence from whence they came. These were also the dead bodies of my knowledge, needs and wants, my desires, my identities for survival over eons on a bedrock of conflicting emotions. I release my outworn connections with survival tactics of past identities. Some say that if you cannot find the secrets of life in love you will find them in pain, if not in beauty, then in violence; lacking inner sight you build bodies from accumulated knowledge, some remarkable, others catastrophic in the effort to find your way.

Returning to the literal sense, in too many religions matter and the body have been forgotten in the effort of upholding Spirit. In the reversed process of working through, rather than ignoring matter, you will find your identity and lessen the extremes that have blighted your religious experience. I have spent lives on your Earth too often, and, at times, too long. Not so long ago, emotionally drained, I waned into tears of exhaustion. I wanted to return to my people. In my misery came a presence that stood behind me in an authority from eons past. The presence I knew was male. He laughed into my distress.

"Who are you?" I cried. "Do I know you?" His voice came clear inside my head. "I am your best friend."

With sadness and indeed horror, I felt how far, on one level, I had sunk into forgetfulness. I felt like some pitiable creature, an ambulating zombie living in a manifestation of harsh density. Mortified, I asked many questions, and, on hearing my Commander's name, my heart cracked. Warped in misery, in the words of your inimitable Elizabethan playwrights, I sat like patience on a monument smiling at grief. I was ridiculous! How close is laughter to tears, or love to hate?

"You will not understand now," he said.

"Don't say that!" I replied loudly, moved to annoyance, "Better tell me it is beyond my imagination while here." I needed excuse for my limitations. Ayesha smiled, inclined his head in respect, and, to my relief, left. His presence, I felt, had been intrusive. I had been observed in my diminished state and was overcome with ineptitude. Had he called me by my name, the Endurer, it would have sounded hollow. Had he too forgotten what it is like to incarnate here? In a following encounter Ayesha told me to write.

I wailed in my excuses. I could not. The task was beyond me. Too complicated, too difficult, too layered. There were things that could not be written.

"Oh!" he said with an unsympathetic laugh. "Trust your instincts and memory.

175

Just write with and without mistakes."

He did not have to verbalize the support I knew he would give, providing I took up my metaphorical kris and got to work, dragging my tale of myth and imagination from all levels of experience in this world that had to be put into words despite inaccuracies and other distortions hardly avoidable while in an Earthling's body of mixed genetic source.

Sometimes I wish to shield myself and excuse my frailty. I have too often incarnated as a woman inextricably bound to my Commander, even in the absence of recall, when living on your blue planet spinning on the edge of the Milky Way.

*Dawn breaks with song in a silvered sky*
*Like an infant's laugh before it can talk*
*Coming with sound and colour unknown*
*Beyond the hues of charcoal to chalk.*

*Keresch song of the young mothers.*

*Myth, mystery, metaphor, and imagination are not confined to time, as you know it.*
*They run through past, present, and future revealing underlying patterns that*
*drive us forward. If you fail to be touched, you will be excluded from the poet's*
*vision and you will remain bound to the limitations of materialism expanded with advanced*
*technology to supply commercially profitable goods to fill your empty souls.*

# Epilogue

How, you may ask, does this tale relate to the here and now of your existence? Your world of the Kali Yuga is upside down, back to front, inside out, and wobbles on the cusp of change, and be there a time to turn the other cheek, then there is also a time to rebel, or you will be slain by the fire and the sword. It is time for an alchemical transfiguration.

In confusion you roam your Internet with its endless chatter, information, proclamations, and diet feeding the needy in preparation for the future, lurking like a hidden serpent waiting to be released from the next coil of a Mayan calendar. Your situation, I reply, is similar to the time when we and other galactic peoples were threatened by Dark Forces seeking our destruction.

Thoughts are things; thoughts influence things. Thoughts with intention and attention become stronger with more people thinking the right thoughts. You have bought into competition and materialism. And it doesn't matter what technology you have, if not used with an awakened consciousness, you will never free yourselves. Empty your minds from the muddle and mess of your world. Open your hearts. Give space for a higher order to move. It is even possible to achieve a criticality. At present unfortunately, so much of your New Age activity is little more than children playing ring-a-ring-o'roses around the crater of a volcano about to explode.

You have a surfeit of barefoot females dancing around Gaia in worship and forgetting the need to educate your men to emotionally give her respect, support, and appreciation as much as they give her technology. Gaia needs male love.

Go into your future, a Promethean journey to reclaim your fire, a potency of celestial origin. Use myth to stimulate your potential of being Heracles with the strength of Titans. Sing with Apollo, the sun god whose song is of magic, harmonic vibration. Fly with joy on the hawk wings of your *BA*. Be lifted beyond the ambivalence of fear and courage. Know that illumination also carries a shadow or you would be blinded by the Light. Will we help? We watch and wait for your actions before we take ours.

The universe breathes carrying the Christ conciousness. A myriad suns explode, and from rivers of light, their dust is carried throughout space; stardust containing the essential elements of your world whirl about you in their dance of life. How often, when analysing matter, you forget that the hydrogen, oxygen, nitrogen, and carbon contained in the microcosm of your physique correspond to the same elements and more, belonging to the macrocosm beyond.

The many-facetted universe is within you and you are within it.


*But all joy wants eternity - Wants deep, wants deep eternity*

*Frederich Nietzsche 1844-1900*

*Life is pure flame and we live
by an inner invisible sun.*

Sir Thomas More 1478-1535

Made in the
USA
Middletown, DE